On the cover:

Ma patrie (2011)
Oil on canvas
Noëlla Richard

Réfugiés de Malpèque
Drawing
Réjean Roy

Illustrated History of the Acadians of Prince Edward Island

Georges Arsenault

Illustrated History of the Acadians of Prince Edward Island

Translated by Sally Ross

The Acorn Press
Charlottetown
2019

ISBN 978-1-77366-043-1

Translation: Sally Ross
Maps: Samuel Arseneault
Design: Guy Vaillancourt
Editing: Elizabeth Eve
Illustrations: Réjean Roy
Printing: Marquis

Library and Archives Canada Cataloguing in Publication

Illustrated history of the Acadians of Prince Edward Island / Georges Arsenault; translated by Sally Ross.

Translation of: Histoire illustrée de l'Acadie de l'Île-du-Prince-Édouard.
Includes bibliographical references.

ISBN 978-1-77366-043-1 ISBN 978-1-77366-044-8 (epub)
Canadiana 20190109866 (print) 20190109874 (ebook)

1. Acadians—Prince Edward Island—History. 2. Acadians—Prince Edward Island—Social life and customs. 3. Prince Edward Island—History.

LCC FC2650.5.A77 2019 DDC 971.7/004114—dc23

The publisher wishes to acknowledge the financial support of the Prince Edward Island Museum and Heritage Foundation for the publication of this book. We also acknowledge the financial support of the Government of Canada and the Canada Council for the Arts for their investment in our publishing activities.

Canadä

Canada Council for the Arts | Conseil des arts du Canada

ACORN PRESS

P.O. Box 22024
Charlottetown, Prince Edward Island C1A 9J2
acornpresscanada.com

Contents

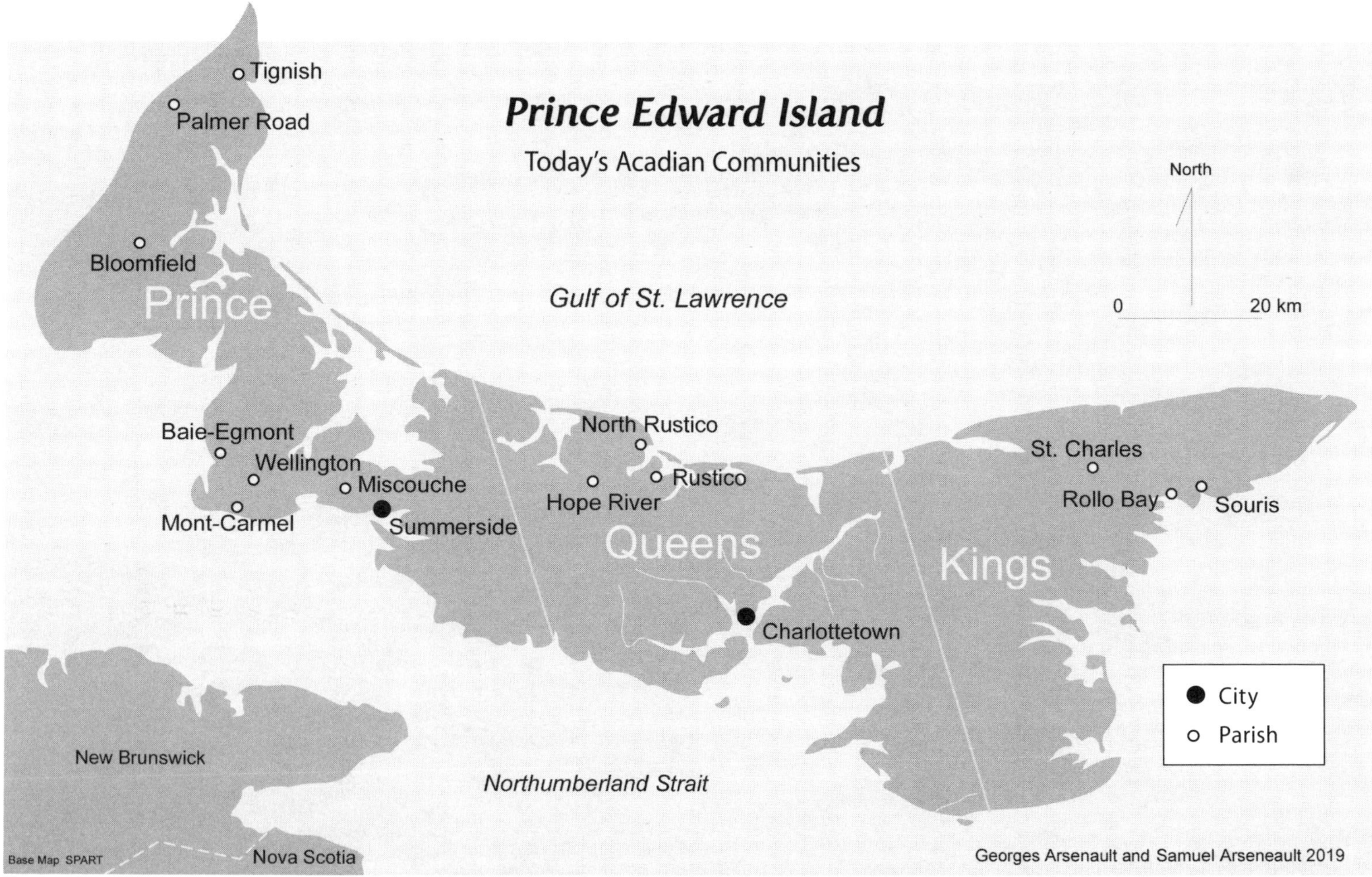
Prince Edward Island
Today's Acadian Communities
Tignish
Palmer Road
Bloomfield
Prince
Gulf of St. Lawrence
North
0
20 km
Baie-Egmont
Wellington
Miscouche
Mont-Carmel
Summerside
North Rustico
Rustico
Hope River
Queens
Charlottetown
St. Charles
Rollo Bay
Souris
Kings
City
Parish
New Brunswick
Northumberland Strait
Nova Scotia
Base Map SPART
Georges Arsenault and Samuel Arseneault 2019

Foreword

The year 2020 marks the 300th anniversary of French and Acadian presence on Prince Edward Island, formerly known as Île Saint-Jean. In 1720, after France founded the colony of Île Saint-Jean, the Island was settled by men and women from France and Acadie. Although the French regime ended with the deportation of the francophone inhabitants by the British in 1758, several families managed to stay on the Island. Therefore, since 1720 there have always been Acadians living in what was to become Canada's smallest province. The French language and Acadian culture have thus been part of the province's heritage for 300 years.

In the decades following the Deportation, the Acadians gradually began the difficult task of rebuilding their community under British rule. Scattered in small settlements from one end of the Island to the other, for a long time they were regarded as a separate people. Little by little, however, the Acadian community emerged from isolation to take its place in the predominantly English-speaking Island society.

The evolution of the different Acadian areas and their ability to retain the French language and their cultural identity varied considerably depending on the size and homogeneity of their population. This is particularly evident, for example, in the case of the Evangeline Region (Egmont Bay, Mont-Carmel, and Wellington) and the eastern Kings County area (Rollo Bay, Souris, and St. Charles). Although the Evangeline Region is not the community with the largest number of Acadians, it is the most ethnically homogeneous, a fact that helped preserve both the French language and its Acadian identity. The eastern Kings area, on the other hand, is not only one of the smallest Acadian communities in the province, but it is also located in a region where the vast majority of the population is of British origin. As a result, it succumbed the most rapidly to anglicization.

The goal of this book is to provide an overview of the history of the Acadians on Prince Edward Island during the past three centuries. It does not tell the story of every Acadian village and parish, but starting with the colonization of the Island by France, the chapters examine the deportation of the inhabitants in 1758, the resettlement of the Island by Acadians in subsequent years, the economic life, the role of the Catholic Church, education in French, and finally the efforts to preserve the French language and culture. The many photographs throughout the book illustrate the richness and vitality of the Acadian community on Prince Edward Island.

Readers who would like to learn more about the history and traditions of Island Acadians will find a selective bibliography at the end of the book that lists articles and books published for the most part since 1980.

It is my hope that this publication will help not only Islanders in general to become more familiar with the Acadian community of Prince Edward Island, but also everyone who is interested in the history of the Acadian people and their contribution to Canada.

Happy reading!

Georges Arsenault

Chapter 1

The Colony of Île Saint-Jean 1720–1758

A great many people living on Prince Edward Island today are descendants of the first Acadian men and women who settled on the Island in the 1720s. They had come from Acadie, a French colony founded in 1604. Although the boundaries of Acadie changed over the years, by 1700 it corresponded roughly to present-day Nova Scotia, excluding Cape Breton Island.

The Acadians settled primarily along the Baie Française (Bay of Fundy) where they cultivated the lowlands and raised livestock. They became relatively prosperous despite the fact that they were living in a politically unstable colony. Because of its strategic location, Acadie was coveted by both the French and the British and changed hands on numerous occasions. As a result, sometimes the Acadians lived under the control of France, sometimes under the control of Great Britain.

France ceded peninsular Acadie to Great Britain for the last time through the Treaty of Utrecht in 1713. The Acadians stayed on their farms in the hope that the territory would once again be returned to France. Meanwhile, French authorities encouraged them to move to Île Royale (Cape Breton Island) where a fortress was being built in Louisbourg that was to become an important military and commercial town. Since fertile land was scarce, only a few Acadians moved to Île Royale. France then decided to establish a colony on Île Saint-Jean where the soil appeared to be much more suitable for agriculture. The idea was to get settlers from Acadie and France to grow crops and raise livestock in order to supply the fortress town of Louisbourg. Given the happy and promising name of Port-la-Joye, the capital of the little colony was established on the shores of the harbour at the mouth of the Island's three main rivers.

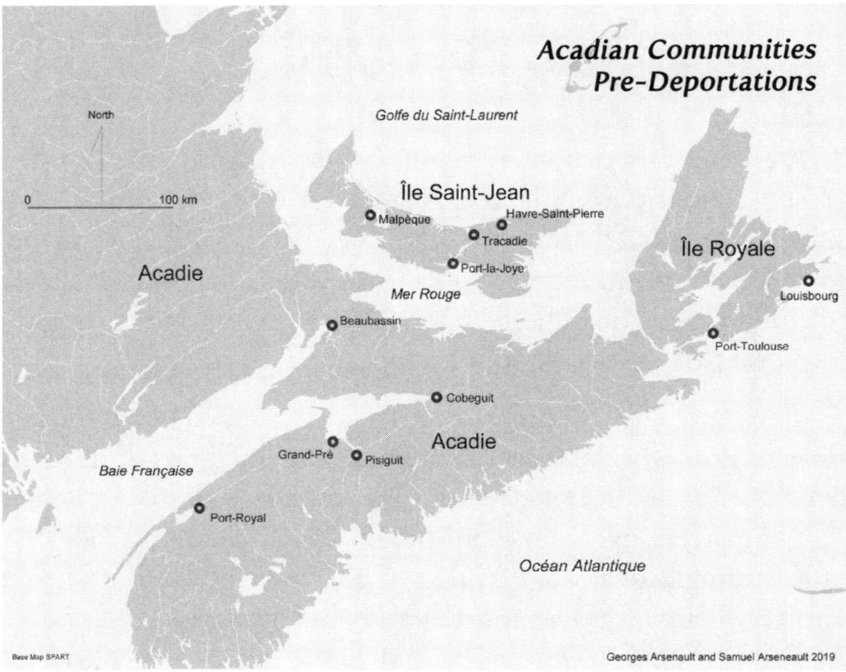

Although Île Saint-Jean was placed under the direct administration of Île Royale, France granted the responsibility of colonizing Île Saint-Jean to a private company appropriately named the Compagnie de l'Île Saint-Jean. The principal shareholder, Louis-Hyacinthe de Castel, Comte de Saint-Pierre, was from Normandy. In the spring of 1720, the company recruited 200 settlers and fishermen in France and brought them to the Island.

The company was more interested in the cod fishery than in agriculture, so most of the settlers were placed in Havre-Saint-Pierre (St. Peter's Harbour) on the north shore, near the fishing banks. For the 38 years of the colony of Île Saint-Jean,

Havre-Saint-Pierre remained the most populated area and the most important centre for the fishery.

It was not long before the Compagnie de l'Île Saint-Jean encountered serious financial difficulties that forced it to abandon the colony in 1724. Most of the people the company had brought to the Island left, but some stayed behind to supply fish to entrepreneurs in Louisbourg and France.

Port-la-Joye

Port-la-Joye was the military and administrative centre of the Île Saint-Jean colony and the location of the living quarters of the Commander, the subdelegate of the Intendant of New France, and several officers in charge of the colonial administration. A garrison of between 25 and 40 soldiers protected the colony against attacks from the British.

A number of buildings were erected over the years, including dwellings for the officers and the chaplain, and barracks for the soldiers. There was also a chapel, a bakery, and a storage depot. Not far from these buildings were the settlers' houses and farms. Until 1745, the village was inhabited primarily by the extended family of Michel Haché (*dit* or also known as Gallant).

The drawing above by the engineer Étienne Verrier the Younger, dated 1734, is part of a plan of a fort intended for Port-la-Joye. The palisade shown was never built. On the left is the village of Port-la-Joye which was inhabited mainly by members of the Haché (or Gallant) family. (LAC, Ph 240, Port La Joye/1734)

Many Acadians today are descendants of the two families that the company enticed to the Island in 1720. Michel Haché (also known as Gallant) and Anne Cormier came from Beaubassin (near present-day Amherst, Nova Scotia), while Pierre Martin and Anne Godin originated from Port-Royal (Annapolis Royal) but had spent several years on Île Royale. Pierre Martin's mother was Aboriginal, as was, perhaps, Michel Haché's. The Haché family settled in Port-la-Joye and the Martin family settled near the Rivière du Nord-Est (Hillsborough River), alongside what is today called the Mount Stewart Marsh.

In the years that followed, other families left Acadie to make their homes on Île Saint-Jean, but, despite encouragement from the French authorities, they were few in number. Even fewer individuals from France put down roots after 1725. According to the 1735 census, not counting the Mi'kmaq, there were 432 inhabitants, 36 per cent of whom were of Acadian descent. They were living in the following settlements: Port-la-Joye, Havre-Saint-Pierre, Tracadie, Havre-aux-Sauvages, Rivière-du-Nord-Est, Malpèque, Trois-Rivières, and Pointe-de-l'Est.

The Mi'kmaq

When the French and Acadians settled on the Island in 1720, it was not uninhabited. It constituted part of the territory called Mi'kma'ki frequented by the indigenous people known as the Mi'kmaq. Mi'kma'ki encompassed what is now Newfoundland, Nova Scotia, Prince Edward Island, the eastern and northern portions of New Brunswick, the Gaspé, and the Magdalen Islands.

The Mi'kmaq adopted the Roman Catholic religion and were allies of the French. They maintained trade ties with the settlers and in the early days of the colonization of Acadie, a number of Frenchmen married Mi'kmaw women. France also established a military alliance with the Mi'kmaq. In fact, almost every summer from 1726 until the early 1740s, the French officials in Port-la-Joye held a large ceremonial gathering attended by Mi'kmaq from the Island and the mainland. During these gatherings, the French gave the Mi'kmaq gifts to thank them for their friendship and to renew their military alliance.

During the French regime, the Mi'kmaw population on the Island was comprised of about 200 individuals. As a nomadic people, they lived from hunting and fishing and usually spent the winter on the mainland in order to hunt moose, an important part of their diet. The French authorities tried unsuccessfully to make the Mi'kmaq settle in one location and to introduce them to farming, encouraging them in particular to establish themselves permanently along the shore of Malpeque Bay.

The surviving parish registers for the period 1720-1758 do not contain any records of marriage between a Mi'kmaq and an Acadian. Thus, despite the friendship between the two groups, cultural differences do not appear to have favoured intermarriages. This has been confirmed by genealogical research.

The population increased gradually although immigration to the Island came to a halt in 1744 with the outbreak of war between France and Great Britain. Both Île Royale and Île Saint-Jean fell to the British who then proceeded to deport the inhabitants of Louisbourg to France. Their plan to deport the population of Île Saint-Jean did not materialize. The Treaty of Aix-la-Chapelle in 1748 brought an end to the war and Great Britain agreed to give back the two island colonies to France. Later that same year, a census indicated that the French and Acadian population of Île Saint-Jean had reached 735 with 128 heads of families.

After the war, fearing deportation, many Acadians under British rule in Nova Scotia felt increasingly vulnerable, so they decided to relocate to Île Saint-Jean. As a result, the population of the Island quadrupled in the space of six years. By 1754 there were almost 3,000 French-speaking inhabitants. The new arrivals moved into the old established settlements and founded many new ones.

The deportation of the Acadians in Nova Scotia to the Anglo-American colonies along the Atlantic coast from Massachusetts to Georgia began in 1755. More than 6,000 men, women, and children were victims of this large-scale deportation organized by the British authorities in Halifax and Boston. Many Acadians managed to escape deportation and hundreds of refugees crossed over to Île Saint-Jean. Their arrival caused a major crisis on the little island colony since most of them were destitute and the authorities lacked the resources to provide them with supplies. Many of them were thus forced to leave for the refugee camp on the Miramichi River, while others made their way to Quebec.

For the Acadian refugees who did stay on the Island, their respite was of short duration. In 1758, after Louisbourg was captured by troops led by General Jeffery Amherst, Île Saint-Jean once again became a British colony. Amherst ordered all the Acadian and French inhabitants on the Island to be rounded up and deported to France. It is estimated that the population was comprised of 4,250 civilians and about 100 soldiers and officials.

Kjiktu'lnu, Epekwitk, Île Saint-Jean, Prince Edward Island

The Mi'kmaq, who had been living on the Island for centuries before the arrival of the French, used very descriptive terms to identify their island home. *Kjiktu'lnu,* for example, means "our great boat" and *Epekwitk* (*Abegweit,* the anglicized form) means "cradled by the waves."

The French no doubt chose the name *Île Saint-Jean* in honour of St. John the Baptist whose feast day falls on June 24. It was often around that date that European fishermen and explorers landed on the shores of North America. It is not known who chose the name *Île Saint-Jean* nor when, but it appears on a map as early as 1601.

Although some writers state that Jacques Cartier named the Island, in fact, when he landed there on his voyage in 1534, he thought it was part of the mainland. He did, however, leave the first written description of the Island: "All this coast is low and flat but it is the finest land one can see, and full of beautiful trees and meadows."

When the British took control of the Island in 1758, they simply translated the French name and called it *St. John's Island* or *Island of St. John.* In 1799, to avoid confusion with other places named after St. John, they decided to call it *Prince Edward Island* in honour of the Duke of Kent, a son of King George III. The official French translation of the name is *Île-du-Prince-Édouard.*

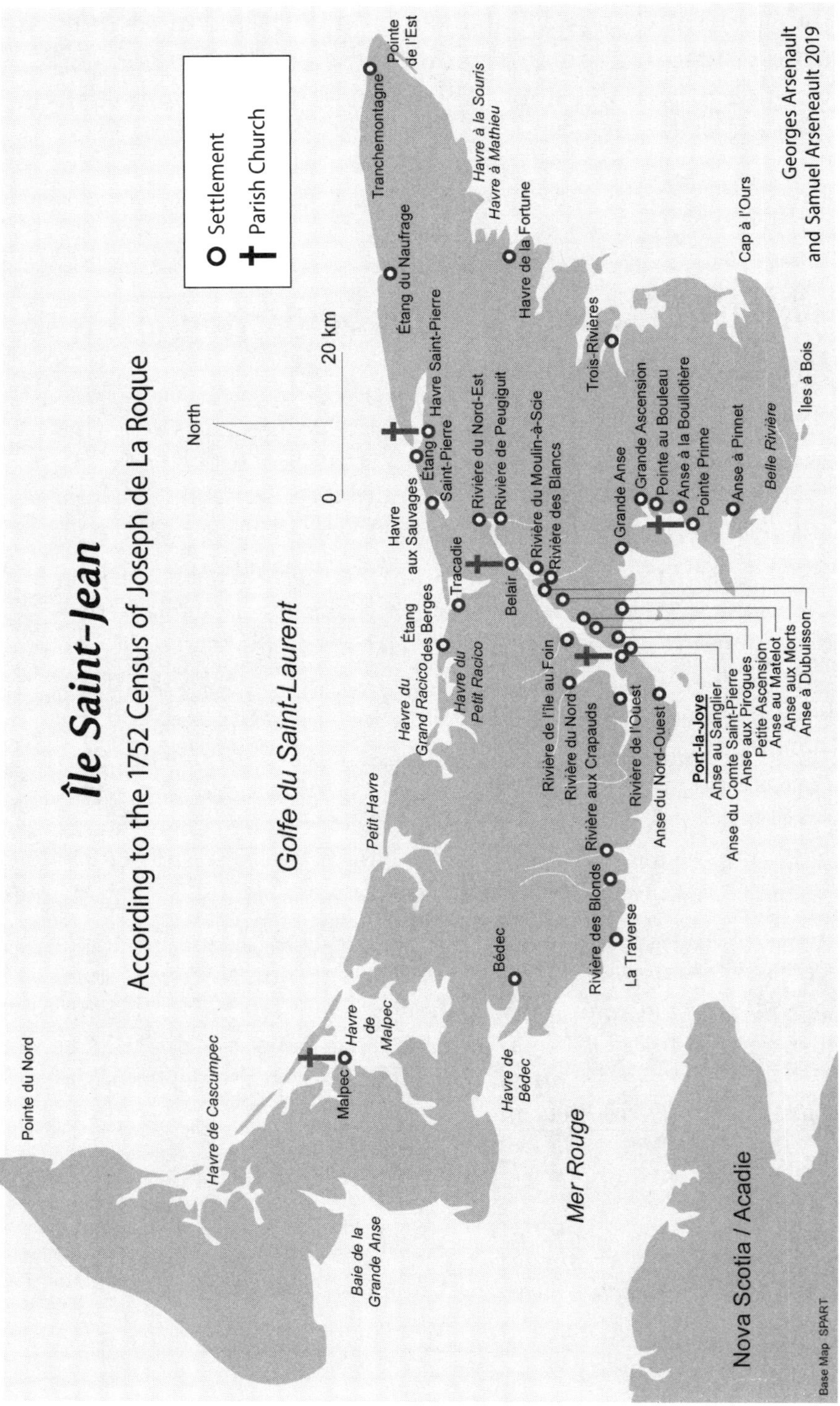

Île Saint-Jean
According to the 1752 Census of Joseph de La Roque
Settlement
Parish Church
North
0
20 km
Golfe du Saint-Laurent
Pointe du Nord
Havre de Cascumpec
Malpec
Havre de Malpec
Baie de la Grande Anse
Havre de Bédec
Bédec
Mer Rouge
Nova Scotia / Acadie
Petit Havre
Havre du Grand Racico
Havre du Petit Racico
Étang des Berges
Tracadie
Havre aux Sauvages
Étang Saint-Pierre
Havre Saint-Pierre
Étang du Naufrage
Tranchemontagne
Pointe de l'Est
Havre à la Souris
Havre à Mathieu
Havre de la Fortune
Cap à l'Ours
Îles à Bois
Belle Rivière
Trois-Rivières
Belair
Rivière du Nord-Est
Rivière de Peugiguit
Rivière du Moulin-à-Scie
Rivière des Blancs
Grande Anse
Grande Ascension
Pointe au Bouleau
Anse à la Boullotière
Pointe Prime
Anse à Pinnet
Rivière de l'île au Foin
Rivière du Nord
Rivière aux Crapauds
Rivière de l'Ouest
Anse du Nord-Ouest
Rivière des Blonds
La Traverse
Port-la-Joye
Anse au Sanglier
Anse du Comte Saint-Pierre
Anse aux Pirogues
Petite Ascension
Anse au Matelot
Anse aux Morts
Anse à Dubuisson
Georges Arsenault and Samuel Arseneault 2019
Base Map SPART

The Families on Île Saint-Jean in 1752

At the request of the Governor of Louisbourg, during the summer of 1752 the surveyor Joseph de la Roque visited all the settlements on Île Saint-Jean to take a census of the population. He enumerated 2,223 inhabitants. The following is a list of the settlements and the names of the families living in each settlement. The modern place names are given in brackets.

SETTLEMENTS	FAMILIES
Anse à Dubuisson (Curry's Cove)	*Barrieau, Boudrot, Doiron, Savary, Vincent* dit *Clément*
Anse à Pinnet (Stewart Cove/Pinette)	*Apart, Aucoin, Boudrot, Dugas, Gautrot, Henry, Landry, Melanson, Michel, Naquin, Pitre*
Anse au Matelot (Alexandra Bay)	*Aucoin, Benoit, Billeray, Cyr, Daigre, Doiron, Guédry, Lavache, Le Blanc, Lejeune, Lucas, Roy, Rullier, Trahan, Vincent* dit *Clément*
Anse au Sanglier (Holland Cove)	*Join, Lecchis, Turcot*
Anse aux Morts (Mermaid)	*Doiron, Thériot*
Anse aux Pirogues (Stewart Cove)	*Hébert, Le Marquis, Michel* dit *Laruine, Vincent*
Anse de la Boullotière (Newtown)	*Henry*
Anse du Comte Saint-Pierre (Keppoch)	*Cyr, Deschamps* dit *Cloche, Gautrot*
Anse du Nord-Ouest (Bacon Cove)	*Brasseur, Gaudet, Nogues*

Bédec (Bédèque)	*Froiquingont, Guédry, Lejeune, Robichaud, Thériot*
Belair (Scotchfort)	*Broussard, Bugeaud, Gauthier*
Étang des Berges (Stanhope)	*Boudrot, Chiasson*
Étang Saint-Pierre (St. Peters Lake)	*Caissie, Grossin, Livois, Ouvray, Quimine*
Grande Anse (Pownal Bay)	*Arsement, Boudrot, Breau, Chauvet, Daigre, Doiron, Hébert, Landry, Leprince, Melanson, Pitre, Raymond, Ségoillot*
Grande Ascension (Scentia Road)	*Benoit, Carret, Dugas, Guérin, Hébert, Henry, Lejeune*
Havre aux Sauvages (Savage Harbour)	*Bourey, Chenêt, Chiasson, Compagnon, de La Foresterie, Delaunay, Deveau, Habel* dit *Duvivier, Pothier, Renaud, Tudal*
Havre la Fortune (Bay Fortune)	*Daigre, Delaune, Durel* dit *Lacroix, Laborde, Le Blanc, Le Prieur*
Havre Saint-Pierre (St. Peters Harbour)	*Bernard, Bertaud* dit *Montaury, Billard, Bonnière, Boudrot, Charpentier, Châtel, Delaborde, Despoués, Douville, Dubois* dit *Dumont, Duboscq, Duplessis, Durocher, Émard de Thézen, Fouquet, Fricond* dit *Picard, Gallet, Hango, Hébert* dit *Manuel, Jacquet, Jolly, Jousseaume, Le Breton, Le Buffe, Legendre, Le Prieur* dit *Dubois, Le Vieux, Loyal, Mancel, Morel, Patry, Renaud, Talbot, Thénière, Viarrieu* dit *Duclos*
Havre Saint-Pierre – rive nord (Greenwich)	*Beaulieu, Detcheverry, Lacroix, Oudy, Vécot*

La Traverse (Cape Traverse)	*Blanchard, Boudrot*
Malpec (Port Hill, Low Point, Birch Hill)	*Arsenault, Blanchard, Boudrot, Comeau, Daigre, DesRoches, Doucet, Dugas, Girouard, Jahan* dit *Laviolette, Le Blanc, Martin* dit *Barnabé, Poirier, Richard*
Petite Ascension (Fullerton's Creek)	*Daigre, Labauve, Poirier, Savary*
Pointe au Bouleau (Birch Point)	*Daigre, Guillot*
Pointe de l'Est (East Point)	*Detcheverry, Pinet*
Pointe Prime (Eldon)	*Arsement, Doiron, Guillot, Henry, Leprince, Pitre*
Port-la-Joye (Rocky Point)	*Benet, Caissie, Cirier, Hébert, Henry, Juineau* dit *Tonisseaux, Maillardet, Nicolas, Périal, Roussin*
Rivière au Crapaud (Crapaud River)	*Bourg*
Rivière des Blancs (Johnstons River)	*Barrieau, Boudrot, Daigre, Doiron*
Rivière des Blonds (Tryon River)	*Bourg, Renaud, Robichaud*
Rivière de l'île au Foin (Wright's Creek)	*Boudrot, Daigre, Pitre*
Rivière de l'Ouest (West River)	*Bourg, Breau, Guérin, Henry, Pitre, Thériot, Thibodeau*
Rivière de Peugiguit (Pisquid)	*Gallon, Girard, Glain* dit *Cadet, Haché* dit *Gallant, Olivier, Poirier, Rassicot, Renaud*

Rivière du Moulin-à-Scie (Glenfinnan River)	*Aucoin, Boisseau, Bugeaud, Caissie, Cellier, Doiron, Gautrot, Hébert, Landry, Le Blanc, Thériot, Thibodeau*
Rivière du Nord (North River)	*Daigre, Landry*
Rivière du Nord-Est (Mount Stewart, St. Andrews)	*Aucoin, Blanchard, Bourg, Darembourg, Deveau, Doiron, Doucet, Dugas, Duguay, Gaudet, Haché* dit *Gallant, Hélie, Langlois, Michel, Philippe* dit *La Roche, Pothier, Prétieux*
Rivière du Nord-Est (Cherry Hill, Allisary)	*Bouchard, Bourgeois, Duval, Haché* dit *Gallant, Martin, Vécot*
Rivière de Peugiguit (Pisquid West)	*Closquinet* dit *Dumoulin, Doucet, Hango, Lucas* dit *Bergerac, Vallée* dit *Langevin*
Tracadie	*Belliveau, Boudrot, Bourg, Haché* dit *Gallant*

Chapter 2

The Deportation

The Deportation of the inhabitants of Île Saint-Jean is unquestionably the most tragic and disastrous event in the Island's history. It took place during the Seven Years' War (1756-1763), a global war that was fought in Europe, India, and North America and also at sea. As rival empires, both Great Britain and France sought supremacy in North America. Great Britain's aim was to take control of all of France's possessions in North America.

In the summer of 1758, British troops attacked the fortress town of Louisbourg, seat of the government on Île Royale. The French surrendered on July 26 and since Île Saint-Jean was a dependency of Île Royale, it was included in the articles of capitulation. Thus, the British authorities decided to deport the population of both islands to France.

Lieutenant Colonel Andrew Rollo was assigned the task of coordinating the takeover of Île Saint-Jean. With a contingent of 500 soldiers, he landed in Port-la-Joye on August 17 and immediately took the French garrison and administrative officials prisoner and began arresting the civilian population. On his arrival, Lord Rollo discovered a fertile island that he felt would be suitable for British settlers. Realizing that the houses could be of use in the future, he decided to not have them destroyed.

Since the British had underestimated the size of the population of Île Saint-Jean, Lord Rollo was forced to request more ships from Louisbourg so that all the island inhabitants could be transported to France. The shortage of vessels slowed down the evacuation process, which meant that many Acadian families were able to avoid deportation by escaping from the Island and taking refuge on the mainland.

Between August 31 and November 4, 1758, approximately 3,000 of the 4,250 inhabitants were deported to France; some of the ships stopped in Louisbourg before starting the transatlantic voyage. Nearly half of the deportees drowned or succumbed to malnutrition or sickness.

Three vessels were shipwrecked: the *Duke William*, the *Violet*, and the *Ruby*. On December 12, the *Violet*, carrying 300 deportees, sank in the English Channel. There were no survivors. The next day, with the exception of four deportees and the priest Jacques Girard, all of the approximately 360 Acadians on board the *Duke William* were lost. On December 16, the *Ruby* ran aground in the Azores, an archipelago off Portugal. Of the 310 Acadian passengers, 190 drowned.

The death toll was high on board the other ships, especially among the 500 passengers on the *Mary*: 255 died during the crossing, most of whom were children. When the ship docked

The Tragedy of the Duke William

The *Duke William*, a 400-tonne ship, was one of the largest transport vessels used to deport the Acadians from Île Saint-Jean. It is estimated that it had 360 passengers, including Father Jacques Girard, priest of Saint-Paul's parish in Pointe-Prime, and a large number of his parishioners.

The fate of the *Duke William* is well known. It left Port-la-Joye on November 4, 1758. During the transatlantic voyage it suffered major damages in severe storms and started taking on water. The *Duke William* sank on December 13, 1758, off the coast of England. The captain, the 34 members of the crew, Father Girard, and four Acadians survived, while all the other passengers who had managed to survive the crossing perished. That day in December was the deadliest day of all the deportations during the period known as the *Grand Dérangement* or the Great Upheaval.

According to the genealogist Stephen A. White, author of the *Dictionnaire généalogique des familles acadiennes*, 11 of the 13 families who were enumerated in Pointe-Prime in the 1752 census were aboard the *Duke William*, about 120 of whom were members of Noël Doiron's family.

Patriarch of Pointe-Prime, Noël Doiron was about 74 years old in 1758. He was the old man described as the "head prisoner" in the detailed account of the last voyage of the *Duke William* written by William Nicholls, the captain. As the following quotation indicates, "the old gentleman" came to speak to the captain on behalf of the other deportees because he knew the ship was going to sink and that there was not enough room in the lifeboats for all the passengers:

> *About half an hour after, the old gentleman came to me, crying; he took me in his arms, and said he came with the voice of the whole people, to desire that I and my men would endeavour to save our lives, in our boats; and as they could not carry them, they would on no consideration be the means of drowning us. They were well convinced, by all our behaviour, that we had done everything in our power for their preservation, but that God Almighty had ordained them to be drowned, and they hoped that we should be able to get safe ashore.*

The survivors of the *Duke William* landed near Penzance on the southwest coast of England. The Pointe-Prime parish priest eventually made his way to France where he was given a permanent position as chaplain at the abbey in Jouarre, not far from Paris, where he died in 1782.

in Portsmouth, England, to replenish the supply of fresh water, Admiralty officials were told that many of the passengers were sick. After investigating, they learned that the high number of deaths during the transatlantic crossing was due to the foul air and the filth in the overcrowded hold. They also noted that the passengers lacked everything, including clothing.

The Acadians who survived the crossing disembarked in French ports, primarily in St. Malo and Boulogne-sur-Mer where local officials took charge of them. Already in poor health, many of the deportees died in the days, weeks, or months that followed. The survivors hoped to return to their lands in the New World once the war was over. This proved impossible since the terms of the Treaty of Paris in 1763 stipulated that France had to relinquish the colonies of Île Saint-Jean, Île Royale, and Canada (Quebec) to Great Britain.

The deportees from Île Saint-Jean in France found themselves with inhabitants from Île Royale along with a group of Acadians who had been deported from Nova Scotia in 1755. By 1763, there was a total of about 3,000 deportees.

According to the Treaty of Paris, France was able to keep the Caribbean islands of Martinique, Guadeloupe, and Santo Domingo, along with Guyana and the Falkland Islands. French officials encouraged the Acadians from Île Saint-Jean, Île Royale, and Nova Scotia to settle in these southern colonies. Quite a few of them went there, but it proved to be a disastrous decision because many succumbed to tropical diseases. Some of the families ended up staying in these colonies, but others left in search of a more hospitable place of refuge.

A number of the Acadian deportees in France decided to return to the Gulf of St. Lawrence, which was now under British control. They were recruited by British merchants who were looking for men to work in the fishery. Only two of the families—the Doirons and the Longuépées—came back to settle permanently on Île Saint-Jean.

The government of Louis XV attempted to find land in France where the Acadian deportees could settle. A number of families went to the island of Belle-Île-en-Mer, off the coast of Brittany, and to the province of Poitou, while others ended up staying in various port cities. The majority of them, however, chose to go to Louisiana. In 1785, approximately 1,600 people left the port of Nantes on board seven ships destined for New Orleans.

Acadians Who Escaped Deportation

About 1,250 of the Île Saint-Jean inhabitants avoided deportation. Several families living along the shores of the Rivière du Nord-Est (Hillsborough River) probably managed to leave the Island before Rollo and his soldiers reached their area. This included the Gauthier, Dugas, Bujeau, and Haché (or Gallant) families who were enumerated by the French in a 1760 census at the Petite Rochelle military and refugee camp on the Restigouche River at the head of Chaleur Bay.

All the families living near Malpeque Bay and Tracadie Bay escaped deportation, as did a few from Étang-des-Berges (Stanhope), Havre-aux-Sauvages (Savage Harbour), and Baie-de-Fortune (Bay Fortune). A number of them were able to make their way to the Camp d'Espérance on the Miramichi River and subsequently to the other refugee camp on the Restigouche River.

A few of the families from Malpeque eventually returned to the Island, including families with the following names: Arsenault, Blanchard, DesRoches, Doucet, and Richard. However, the majority of the inhabitants of Malpeque settled elsewhere, often after several moves. They ended up in various places, including the Gaspé peninsula, southeast New Brunswick, Cape Breton Island, the Magdalen Islands, Miquelon, Louisiana, and even in France.

It would appear that a number of families did not leave the Island in 1758. Their names were Boudreau, Bourque, Chiasson, Cormier, Daigle, LeBlanc, and Pitre. According to oral tradition, several of these families were not taken on board the transport ships leaving for France because they had smallpox, a very contagious disease.

Did you know?

- In 1755, there were approximately 14,100 Acadians living in the territory covered by the present-day Maritime provinces. It is estimated that 11,000 Acadians were deported by the British between 1755 and 1762.
- Nearly half of the victims of the deportations were children under the age of 15.
- No Acadians were deported to Louisiana. The first Acadians went there in 1764, nine years after the beginning of the deportations.
- The vast majority of the inhabitants of Île Saint-Jean who were deported to France left in 1785 to settle in Louisiana.

Following the Trail of a Few Deportees

Paul Henry et Théotiste Thibodeau

Paul and his wife Théotiste, from l'Anse-à-Pinet, were 35 and 33 years old, respectively, at the time of the Deportation. They had six children between the ages of one and twelve. The British boat they boarded left Port-la-Joye on November 4, 1758, and dropped anchor 80 days later in the French port of St. Malo. During the rough crossing the couple lost their five youngest children. The tragedy continued after they disembarked in France. Théotiste took her last breath on March 12, 1759, and then Athanase, the only child who had survived the crossing, died several weeks later on April 1. Paul left this world on April 16.

Marie-Josèphe Morel

In 1758, the 60-year-old widow Marie-Josèphe Morel was living in the Havre-Saint-Pierre area. Along with her three sons, Georges, Louis, and Joseph, she was deported across the Atlantic Ocean on the *Supply*. They arrived in St. Malo on March 9, 1759.

Marie-Josèphe and her sons stayed in the St. Malo area until April 20, 1764. She then decided to go with her son, Louis, his wife, Françoise, and their baby to Guyana in South America. The voyage lasted four months. After arriving at their destination, they were placed in temporary, overcrowded lodgings. There was a shortage of food and many of the Acadians succumbed to disease. Marie-Josèphe Morel died November 12, 1764, three months after her arrival in Guyana.

Charles-Olivier Guillot

Charles-Olivier was 11 years old when he was deported to France along with his parents, three sisters, and two brothers. During the transatlantic crossing, he lost his father, both his brothers, and two of his sisters.

He arrived in St. Malo on January 23, 1759, with his mother and his sister, Marie-Josèphe. Charles-Olivier grew up in the St. Malo area and became a carpenter. At the age of 19, he married Madeleine Boudreau, also an Acadian deportee in France. They had four children. In 1775, Charles-Olivier and his family moved to Châtellerault in the province of Poitou, where they stayed for 10 years. Then they made their way to the port of Nantes and sailed to Louisiana along with many other Acadians in 1785. They settled on the Bayou Lafourche.

Alexis Doiron et Madeleine Bourg

The Doiron family from Grande-Anse were transported to France with their five children. During the voyage across the Atlantic, two of the children died and Madeleine gave birth to a boy who died several months later.

The surviving members of the family spent about 10 years in France during which time Madeleine gave birth to eight children. They settled in Saint-Énogat, near St. Malo, then in 1765 they moved to Belle-Île-en-Mer, an island off the coast of Brittany. In 1772, Alexis took his family back to Île Saint-Jean. Along with other Acadians, he settled in Trois-Rivières to work as a fisherman and woodsman for the entrepreneur, David Higgins. Ten years later, he and his family moved to Rustico. They are the ancestors of all the Doirons living on Prince Edward Island today.

The Acadian Odyssey Monument commemorating the Deportation of the Acadians from Île Saint-Jean was unveiled on December 13, 2008, at Skmaqn–Port-la-Joye–Fort-Amherst National Historic Site.

Photo: Georges Arsenault

Chapter 3

Returning to the Island

Despite the fact that the British captured Île Saint-Jean in 1758 and attempted to deport all the inhabitants (except for the Mi'kmaw population), a few families managed to stay on the Island. A number of Acadians who had taken refuge on the mainland along the shores of the Red Sea (Northumberland Strait) and Chaleur Bay returned to the Island even before the treaty ending the war between France and Great Britain was signed in 1763. Most of them were families who had avoided the Deportation of 1758, but there were also a few families who had escaped the Deportation of 1755 and who were living in the Beaubassin area (between present-day Amherst, Nova Scotia, and Sackville, New Brunswick).

These families were not coming back to go into hiding, but rather to earn their livelihoods as fishermen for British entrepreneurs who were operating the commercial cod fishery. Other entrepreneurs were recruiting men to work in the woods. Having lost their ancestral lands, Acadians were thus able to find a certain degree of security and a source of income so they could feed their families.

According to a list compiled in 1763, there were 199 Acadians or 38 families living in six different locations on the Island: Havre-Saint-Pierre, Baie-de-Fortune, Tracadie, Moulin-à-Vent (near present-day Cherry Hill), Rustico, and Port-la-Joye. The same list indicates that 85 Acadians, or 16 households, were living on the Magdalen Islands where the men were hired for the sea cow (walrus) hunt. Since the families were originally from Île Saint-Jean, most of them returned there after a few years.

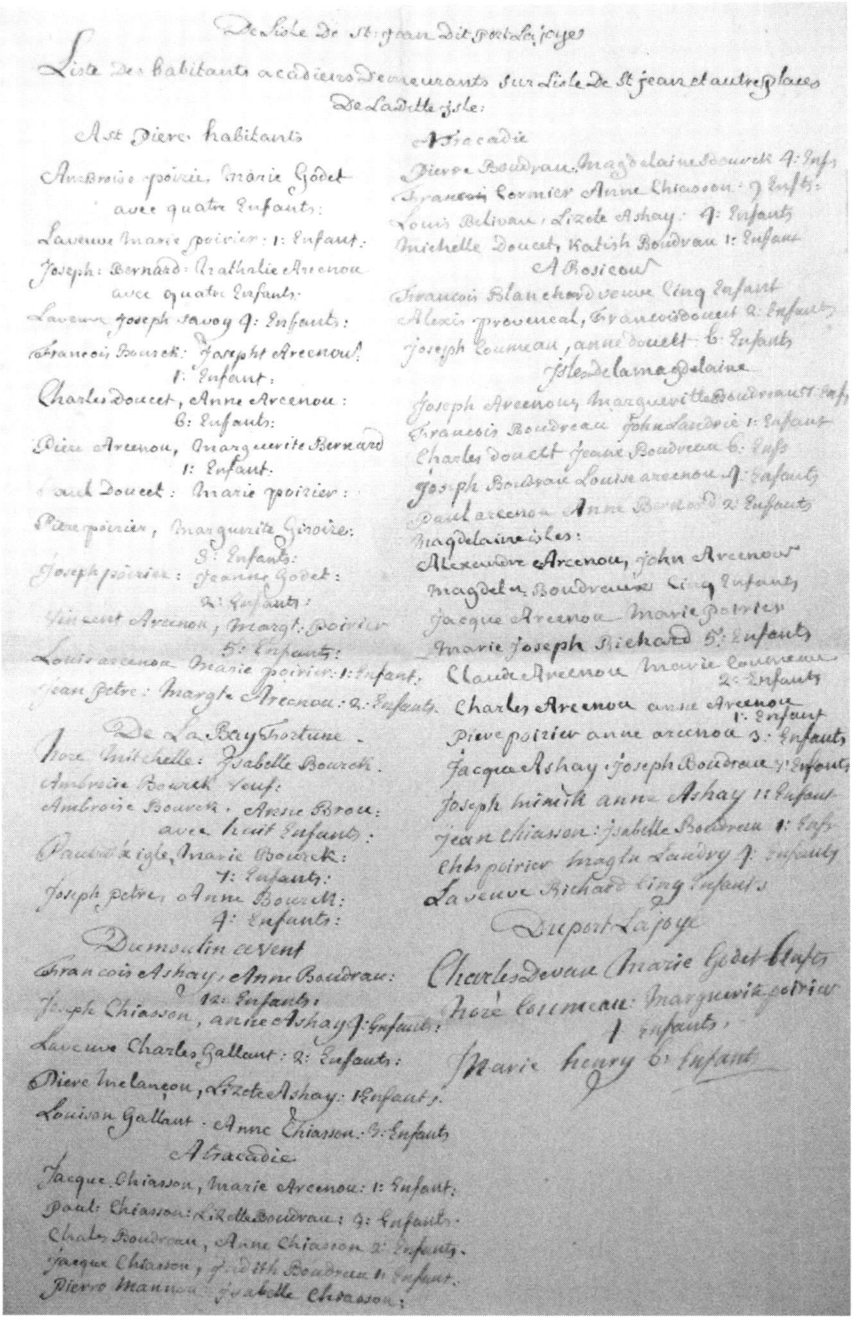

De Lisle de St jean dit Port la joye

Liste des habitants acadiens demeurants sur Lisle de St jean et autres places de Ladite isle:

A St Piere habitants

Ambroise poirie, marie Godet avec quatre Enfants:
La veuve marie poirier: 1: Enfant.
Joseph: Bernard: nathalie Arcenou avec quatre Enfants.
La veuve Joseph Savoy 4: Enfants:
Francois Bourck: Joseph Arcenou 1: Enfant:
Charles Doucet, Anne Arcenou: 6: Enfants:
Pierre Arcenou, marguerite Bernard 1: Enfant.
Paul Doucet: marie poirier:
Pierre poirier, marguerite Giroire: 3: Enfants:
Joseph poirier: Jeanne Godet: 2: Enfants:
Vincent Arcenou, margt: poirier 5: Enfants:
Louis arcenou marie poirier: 1: Enfant.
Jean Petre: margte Arcenou: 2: Enfants.

De La Bay Fortune

Honoré Mitchelle: Isabelle Bourck.
Ambroise Bourck veuf:
Ambroise Bourck. Anne Brou: avec huit Enfants:
Paulin Eigle, marie Bourck: 7: Enfants:
Joseph Petre, Anne Bourck: 4: Enfants:

Dumoulin a vent

Francois Ashay, Anne Boudrau: 12: Enfants:
Joseph Chiasson, anne Ashay 7: Enfants:
La veuve Charles Gallant: 2: Enfants:
Pierre Melançon, Lizette Ashay: 1 Enfant:
Louison Gallant. Anne Chiasson: 3: Enfants

A Tracadie

Jacque Chiasson, marie Arcenou: 1: Enfant.
Paul Chiasson: Lizette Boudrau: 4: Enfants.
Chles Boudrau, Anne Chiasson 2: Enfants.
Jacque Chiasson, Judith Boudrau 1: Enfant.
Pierre Mannon Isabelle Chiasson:

A Tracadie

Pierre Boudrau, magdelaine Doucet 4: Enfs
Francois Cormier Anne Chiasson: 7 Enfs:
Louis Belivau, Lizette Ashay: 4: Enfants
Michelle Doucet, Katish Boudrau 1: Enfant

A Rosicou

Francois Blanchard veuve Cinq Enfant
Alexis provencal, Francoise Doucet 2: Enfants
Joseph Coumeau, anne Doucet 6: Enfants

Isles de la magdelaine

Joseph Arcenou, marguerite Boudreau 7 Enfs
Francois Boudreau Johanne Landrie 1: Enfant
Charles Doucet Jeanne Boudreau 6: Enfs
Joseph Boudrau Louise arcenou 4: Enfants
Paul arcenou Anne Bernard 2: Enfants
magdelaine isles:
Alexandre Arcenou, John Arcenou
magdelen Boudreau Cinq Enfants
Jacque Arcenou marie Poirier
marie Joseph Richard 5: Enfants
Claude Arcenou marie Coumeau 2: Enfants
Charles Arcenou anne Arcenou 1: Enfant
Pierre poirier anne arcenou 3: Enfants
Jacque Ashay Joseph Boudrau 7: Enfants
Joseph minick anne Ashay 11 Enfants
Jean Chiasson: Isabelle Boudreau 1: Enfs
Chles poirier magle Landry 4: Enfants
La veuve Richard Cinq Enfants

Duport Lajoye

Charles Doiron marie Godet 6 Enfs
Honoré Coumeau: marguerite poirier 1 Enfants.
Marie henry 6 Enfant

The 1763 list of Acadians living in six localities on St John's Island and on the Magdalen Islands. This document is in the National Archives of France. (Archives nationales de France. Fonds d'Estaing, 562 AP 16)

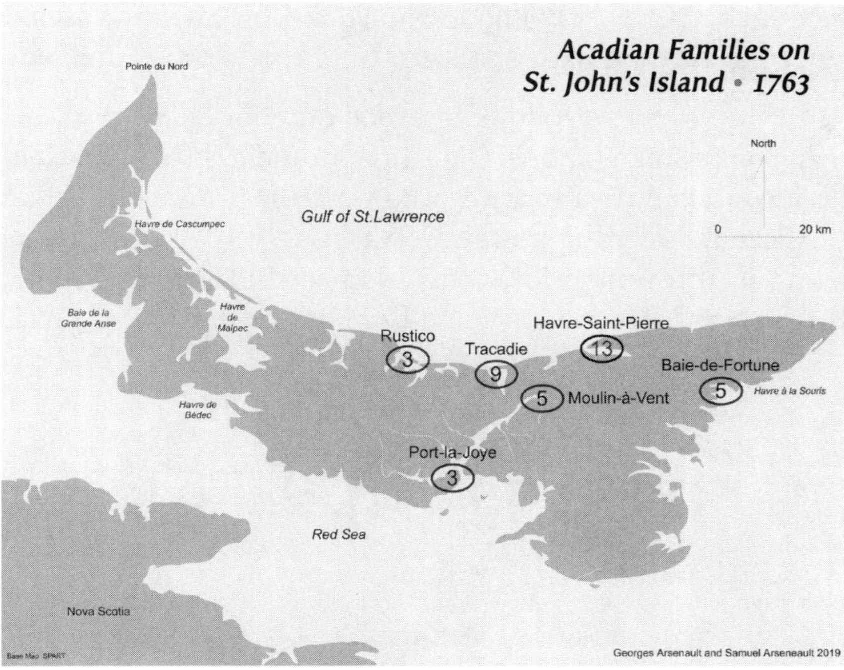

When the surveyor Samuel Holland arrived to survey the Island in the fall of 1764, he and his men discovered that the Acadians were destitute and had moved inland to take shelter in the woods for the winter. He wrote the following:

> The Accadians now have recourse to little Cabbins or Huts in the Woods where they are screened from the violence of the weather and at the same time have the convenience of wood for fuel so near them. Here they live upon Fish they have cured in the Summer, and other game which they frequently kill, as Hares, Partridges, Lynxes or Wild Cats, Otters, Martins or Musk Rats, none of which they refuse to eat as their necessities press them.

A number of the families whose names are on the 1763 list decided to leave the Island. During the 1760s, several moved to the island of Miquelon, some went to the Chaleur Bay area, others to what is now southeastern New Brunswick, and a few to Canada (Quebec). Those who stayed on St John's Island agreed to take the oath of allegiance to the King of England.

In the years that followed, several other families who were living on the mainland, in Cape Breton, and even in Miquelon, decided to join their relatives who were already established on the Island. According to the 1798 census, 682 Acadians were living in three main locations: Malpeque in Prince County, Rustico in Queens County, and Bay Fortune in Kings County.

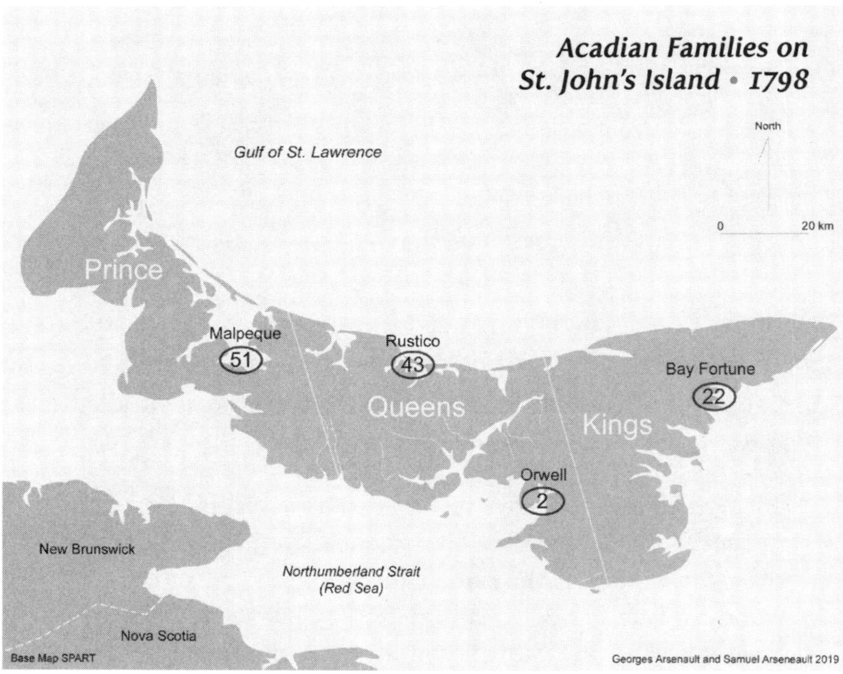

The 1798 Census

Acadian Households

Malpèque	Rustico	Baie-de-Fortune	Orwell
15 Arsenault	12 Gallant	6 Chiasson	2 Cheverie
10 Gallant	6 Martin	6 Bourque	
6 Poirier	5 Pitre	4 Pitre	
4 Bernard	3 Doiron	3 Longuépée	
3 Doucet	3 Doucet	1 Cheverie	
3 Gaudet	2 Blanchard	1 Michel	
2 Chiasson	1 Chiasson	1 Landry	
2 Richard	1 Gautreau		
1 Bourque	1 Lebrun		
1 DesRoches	1 Muise		
1 Downing	1 Buote		
1 Aucoin	1 Gaudet		
1 Roussel	1 Pineau		
1 St-Jean	1 LeClair		
	1 Blaquière		
	1 Gauthier		
	1 DesRoches		

A Large Pioneer Family

In 1728 François Boudrot (nicknamed Manne) and Jeanne Landry settled in Tracadie Bay with their nine daughters and three sons. Several members of the family escaped to the mainland at the time of the Deportation in 1758, but other members, including the parents, appear to have stayed on the Island.

In 1763, François and Jeanne were living on the Magdalen Islands with two of their sons and six of their married daughters. Their four other children were also married but were living on Île Saint-Jean. The men on the Magdalens hunted walrus for Richard Gridley, a merchant from Boston.

By about 1780, the members of this large family were scattered in five different settlements: Malpeque, Rustico, and Bay Fortune on Île Saint-Jean, in Cocagne on the mainland, and on the Magdalen Islands. The majority of Island Acadians today have at least one of the Boudrot daughters in their family tree.

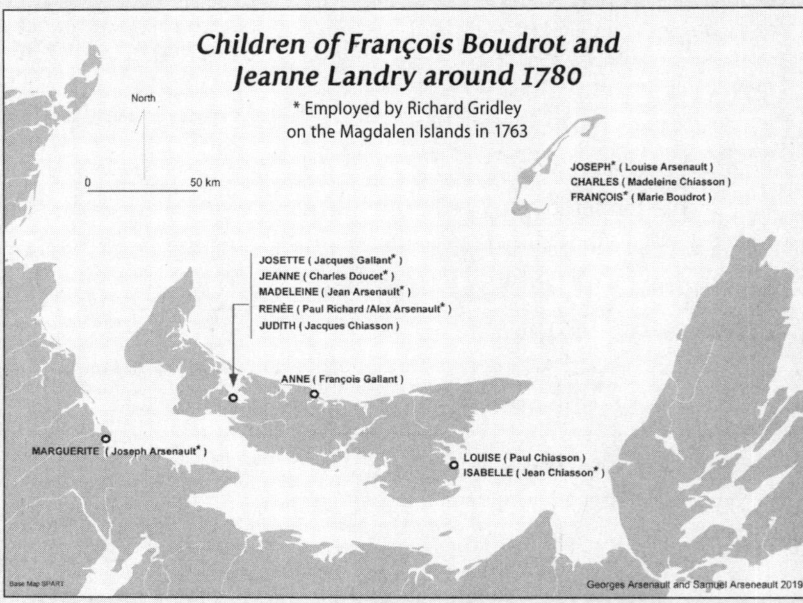

Life as Tenant Farmers

The resettlement of Acadians on Île Saint-Jean, renamed St. John's Island and later Prince Edward Island, proved to be very difficult. By 1765, the surveyor Samuel Holland had divided the Island into 67 townships or lots that were granted in 1767 to deserving British men. As a result, the Acadians were forced to become tenants. Since they were illiterate and had no economic or political influence and few, if any, educated leaders, the Acadians were exploited by these landlords and their agents. The same was true for many of the settlers who arrived from Scotland and Ireland.

This situation explains why, beginning in 1799, numerous Acadian families had to leave the land they were renting and start again elsewhere. The families who had settled in Malpeque Bay moved to Tignish, Cascumpec, Mont-Carmel, Egmont Bay, and Miscouche. Those who were living in Bay Fortune left for Rollo Bay and Cape Breton Island. Some families in Rustico also went to Cape Breton and to Saint-Alexis-de-Matapédia (Quebec).

As early as the 1810s, a number of Acadians managed to become landowners. After Prince Edward Island joined Confederation in 1873, with the help of the federal government, the Province was able to purchase lots that were still owned by large landowners. People were thus able to obtain land more easily. Families living in Rustico took advantage of the opportunity to buy land from the government in St. Charles, Kings County, and in Bloomfield, Prince County.

The Island, being relatively small, had a scarcity of land available for new settlers, especially in the areas where the Acadians had settled. They had large families so it was hard to provide land for the younger generation. Fathers often had to subdivide their property in order to accommodate at least some of their children. Eventually the only solution was to look for land in a neighbouring province. In the second half

Map of Rollo Bay from the *Illustrated Historical Atlas of the Province of Prince Edward Island* (1880). Starting in 1803, the following Acadian families settled there: Daigle (Deagle), Bourque (Burke), LeBlanc (White), Chiasson, Chevarie, Pitre (Peters), Charpentier (Carpenter).

of the 19th century and at the beginning of the 20th century, many young families moved to New Brunswick, specifically to Rogersville, Saint-Paul-de-Kent, and Adamsville, and to the Matapedia Valley in Quebec. Around the same time there was an outmigration to New England where plenty of jobs were available in the factory towns and the forest industry. A significant number of Acadian men and women in search of employment also moved to Summerside and Charlottetown where they were hired as labourers and maids.

The historic Doucet House in Rustico. The first owner, Jean Doucet, was originally from Malpeque. During the years of the Great Upheaval, he moved to the Chaleur Bay area, to Tracadie (Île Saint-Jean) and then to Miquelon where he married Marguerite Gaudet in 1767. From Miquelon, the couple went to Isle Madame in Cape Breton before settling permanently in Rustico around 1772. (Photo: Georges Arsenault)

An Injustice

William Cooper founded and led an unofficial party advocating the confiscation of the large landowners' properties on Prince Edward Island. He defended the Acadians who were being exploited by these men. On March 2, 1844, he published an article in the *Colonial Herald* outlining very clearly how the landowners profited from the Acadians. The following is an extract from his article.

> *The remnant of the Acadian French were allowed to take the Oath of Allegiance; were encouraged to settle themselves, on the promise of protection in person and property by British Officers then in command. The Acadians were left undisturbed until British Emigrants arrived, when Grantees ordered the Acadians to pay rent or give up their improvements, because they were not Foreign Protestants. They chose the latter, and bought unimproved land from another Grantee. Thus both Grantees gained by the transfer; the one gained the value of the Acadians' improvements, and an annual rent for his land, and the other Grantee gained a number of settlers, a high price for his land, and interest upon the purchase money.*

Chapter 4

Economic Life

Farming and fishing were the mainstays of the colony of Île Saint-Jean and continued for a long time to dominate the economic life of the Acadians.

The first fishermen arrived directly from France as employees of the Compagnie de l'Île Saint-Jean. They fished for cod, the most valuable commercial catch. Havre-Saint-Pierre became the main fishing centre and the most populated area on the Island. After the collapse of the company, some of the fishermen were employed by local merchants, while others remained independent and sold their fish to merchants from Louisbourg and France. Every year, numerous young fishermen recruited in France came to spend the summer in Havre-Saint-Pierre. In 1734, for example, 163 Frenchmen were fishing for cod which they salted and dried on the shore.

Fish-House and Stage and Fishing Boats, Rustico. (*Harper's New Monthy Magazine*, 1877)

Life was particularly difficult for the heads of families who relied entirely on fishing. Since they were living a long way from the main settlements, the cost of fishing gear, food and clothing was exorbitant and the price they received for their cod was low. Consequently, they were almost always in debt. The men who were able to combine fishing and farming did somewhat better.

The vast majority of Acadians who moved from Nova Scotia to Île Saint-Jean were farmers. By encouraging them to settle on the Island, France hoped to have an agricultural colony that would meet the needs of Louisbourg. In addition to raising livestock, the settlers grew wheat, peas, turnips, and cabbage. According to the census of 1752, the population of Acadian and French inhabitants totalled 2,223 and their livestock was comprised of 100 horses, 800 oxen, 1,300 other cattle, 1,200 sheep, 1,300 pigs, 2,300 hens, 300 geese, 100 turkeys, and 12 ducks.

Harvesting oats. Village Historique Acadien, Bertrand, N.B.

The same 1752 census indicates that over 1,000 acres were already cleared, but, because of the lack of seed grain, only between 600 and 700 acres were seeded that year. On several occasions during the thirty-eight years the colony of Île Saint-Jean existed, crops were destroyed by forest fires, drought, and infestations of mice and grasshoppers. As a result, the little colony was often forced to turn to Louisbourg for supplies in order to survive. In addition, the impoverished Acadian refugees, who arrived in large numbers in the final years of the colony, were not able to get settled properly and contribute to agricultural production. The Deportation put an end to the plan of making Île Saint-Jean a source of food for Louisbourg.

The Acadians on the Island in the years immediately after the Deportation fished and had vegetable gardens. The men were hired as fishermen by the British cod merchants. During the American War of Independence in the 1770s, all commercial fishing of any importance on the Island came to

Grain Banks

In the early 1860s, Acadian farmers in Prince Edward Island introduced grain banks. They were modelled on regular banks except that all the transactions (shares, interest rates, and dividends) were calculated in bushels of grain. In 1868, the Legislative Assembly of Prince Edward Island passed a law permitting the incorporation of these agricultural banks.

These institutions were a great help to farmers who were often obliged to sell their entire crop of oats in the fall in order to pay their debts. When the time came in the spring to buy their seeds, they had to borrow money from the merchants at interest rates of 50 percent or even 100 percent.

Community grain banks made life much easier for farmers. Those who had the means could invest their surplus crops in the bank. In the spring, those who had to purchase seed grain could borrow from the grain bank at an interest rate of 25 percent. In other words, when they harvested their crop, they had to reimburse the bank five bushels for every four bushels borrowed.

In 1880, there were twenty-four grain banks on the Island, all but one were in Acadian communities. Most of them ceased their operations before 1920, mainly because of improvement in the quality of seeds available on the market. The Urbainville grain bank was the last to close its doors, when the association in charge was dissolved in 1946.

William Perry harvesting grain in Palmer Road, around 1938.
(Rita Perry Collection)

a halt due to the general state of insecurity. So, without completely abandoning the sea, the Acadians devoted themselves more to farming. They caught cod, mackerel, herring, salmon, eels, and other fish for their own consumption and for the local markets. By about 1800, the Acadians owned most of the boats on the Island.

Eventually, the Acadians started clearing and farming the land they were renting. A portion of the quit-rents owed to the large landowners was paid in kind. In Lot 17, for example, Harry Compton's tenants, who occupied 100-acre farms, had to pay him an annual quit-rent of ten bushels of wheat, one sheep, and a certain amount of cash.

For generations, Acadians were subsistence farmers, but nevertheless, despite fairly widespread poverty, they managed well with the bare minimum and enjoyed good health. In 1851 John Lawson, a Charlottetown lawyer, claimed that Acadians were able to raise large families on what would be scarcely enough for one Englishman to live on!

The fishing industry started to make a comeback in the 1840s. By 1852, Tignish was exporting more gaspereau, cod, mackerel, and herring than any other port on the Island. The fish companies that established themselves in Acadian communities like Tignish could find experienced fishermen and workers locally. This resurgence of the fishery occurred just when the younger generation of Acadians was beginning to have difficulties obtaining farm land.

Tignish Run in 1923. (Tignish Arts Foundation Collection)

Fish and Fish Oil Exported from Tignish in 1852

Gaspereau	244 barrels
Cod	2,113 quintals
Hake	167 quintals
Herring	115 barrels
Mackerel	383 barrels
Fish oil	21 barrels

The lobster fishing industry on the Island developed in the 1870s. In 1871, 6,711 pounds of lobster were canned, but eleven years later the amount had reached five million pounds! It was not long before the lobster fishery overtook the commercial cod, mackerel and herring fisheries.

This new industry had a major impact on the Acadian communities: small canneries opened everywhere, providing seasonal work for men and women. The men caught the lobster and the women worked in the canneries. These jobs offered a rare opportunity for women of all ages to earn a salary in or near their own village.

The 1920s ushered in the cooperative movement among Acadian fishermen on the Island. By creating "unions" (precursors of actual cooperatives), they were able to gain a certain degree of control of their industry. They managed their own fish-processing plants and negotiated a better price for their catch, which meant a vast improvement in their standard of living.

The Farmers' Bank of Rustico

The Acadians on Prince Edward Island were the first in Canada to have a people's bank: the Farmers' Bank of Rustico was founded in 1861, and incorporated in 1864 thanks to the initiative of Father Georges-Antoine Belcourt, the energetic parish priest in Rustico. It is the smallest chartered bank that ever existed in Canada and was the precursor of the credit union movement that Alphonse Desjardins started in the province of Quebec in 1900.

When Father Belcourt created this bank, his intention was to develop a spirit of thriftiness and entrepreneurship among his parishioners so that they could have more control over the local economy. At the time, ordinary people did not have access to commercial banks. If they wanted to borrow money, they had to take out loans with merchants or with large landowners who charged exorbitant interest rates.

Having their own bank meant that the Acadians in Rustico could borrow money more easily, so they could purchase land or keep the land they owned. In the spring, they were also able to get loans to buy seed grain. The interest rates varied between six and eight percent. Administered by Acadian farmers, the bank was open on Wednesday afternoons, at which time the twelve elected directors would meet to examine requests for loans.

The Farmers' Bank of Rustico operated successfully for thirty years, in other words until its charter expired in 1894. It was the first cooperative enterprise in the credit sector in Canada.

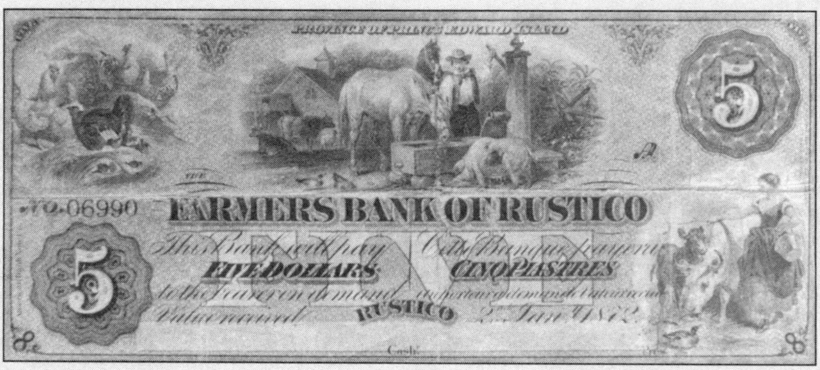

Employees at the lobster canning factory belonging to the Egmont Bay Fishermen's Union in Abram-Village, 1938. (Denise Arsenault Collection)

Despite the size of the lobster fishery, it is important to note that until after the end of the Second World War, the economy in most Acadian communities on the Island was still based on farming. The farms were small and often located in poorly drained lowlands. By around 1940, the average Acadian farmer owned about 60 acres of which about 45 were cultivated: approximately 20 acres in clover and millet, 4 in row crops (turnips, fodder beets, and corn), 16 in oats and mixed grains, and 5 in potatoes. The remaining 15 acres were used as pasture.

Angéline Gaudet collecting eggs in her farmyard in Miscouche. (Armand Arsenault Collection)

Nowadays, very few Acadians earn their living in the agricultural sector.

Alphonse and Marie-Anne Gaudet's farm in St. Nicholas. (Mike Gaudet Collection)

Like other Islanders, they have long since abandoned their mixed farms. With the advent of mechanization and modern farming practices, small family farms were no longer profitable. In addition, most Acadian farmers lacked the capital necessary to adapt to the changes.

The Acadians who have remained in the agricultural sector operate large farms. They bought or rent land vacated by their neighbours and have specialized, opting mostly for dairy farming which provides relative stability because of milk quotas. Others are beef producers or large scale potato producers.

Fishing, on the other hand, constitutes an important part of the economy of many Acadian communities on the Island with lobster being by far the most lucrative catch.

The Gradual Diversification of the Economy

Even though farming formed the basis of the economy in the Acadian communities from 1760 to 1860, this did not prevent Acadians from taking up other trades in order to meet their basic needs. This was particularly necessary when the farms had to be subdivided to accommodate the younger generations. Income from the small farms was not sufficient to provide for large families. In addition, if the families were renting the land, they had to pay their lease.

From the Spirit of Cooperation to the Cooperative Movement

Cooperation has played an important role in the economic life of Island Acadians. Because of the ethnic, linguistic, religious, and socio-economic homogeneity of their villages, Acadians have developed a remarkable spirit of self-help. In the 1860s, they started creating cooperative associations, like the Farmers' Bank of Rustico and the grain banks. Other forms of agricultural cooperatives were also established such as farmer-owned cheese factories, egg circles, and buyers' clubs. In 1909, the first cooperative fish cannery in the province was established by thirty-nine fishermen from North Rustico.

The cooperative movement grew considerably during the difficult years of the Great Depression in the 1930s. The creation of credit unions constituted one of the most impressive initiatives. The concept was well received in the Acadian milieu and helped develop not only a sense of thriftiness, but also financial administrative skills. A group of men and women in Mont-Carmel, for example, founded the Caisse populaire l'Acadienne in 1937. In the early years, the members would meet the manager of the credit union in the presbytery or the parish hall before Sunday mass, so they could deposit their weekly savings of 25 or 50 cents. This little credit union operated successfully until 1969 when it amalgamated with the ones in Egmont Bay and Wellington-Richmond to form the Evangeline Credit Union.

Although constantly evolving to adapt to changes in life style and business, cooperatives are still a very important aspect of the economy in several Acadian regions on Prince Edward Island. While the cooperatives of the past were designed above all to meet the needs of farmers and fishermen, nowadays they are much more diversified and offer services in a wide variety of sectors. Today, for example, there are cooperatives in housing, tourism, handcrafts, and health services.

Évangéline-Central Credit Union, Wellington. (Photo: Jean-Paul Arsenault)

The necessity of finding an income from various sources was very apparent in the case of the Acadians in Rustico, as John MacGregor, an Island landowner and politician, noted around 1820. He wrote that "at one time they are employed in building vessels, at another for a few weeks farming, then fishing, again cutting timber."

Along with farming, boat building and seafaring played an important role in the local economy amongst the Acadians of Rollo Bay, for example. Many men found jobs in near-by shipyards while others were hired as captains or sailors on vessels employed in the shipping trade.

Captain Alphonse Doucette and his son William aboard the schooner *Florence* in Rusticoville around 1923. The schooner was owned by the Rustico merchant, Joseph Gallant. (Paula Gauthier Collection)

In his book called *Letters on Prince Edward Island*, published in 1851, John Lawson describes Acadians as hard-working people and excellent labourers. He also states that they showed a love for fishing. In his opinion, the Acadian population was an asset to the Island because it provided a skilled, cheap workforce.

Business People

Throughout the French regime, a number of merchants conducted business in the colony of Île Saint-Jean. The census takers refer to them as *négociants*, in other words merchants or traders. For the most part they were involved with the fishery as agents for companies who bought fish from the fishermen and sold them fishing gear, food, clothing, and alcohol.

In 1752, there were six merchants on the Island, one of whom was the Acadian Marie Allain, widow of the trader Nicolas Gautier. She and one other merchant were living in Rivière-du-Nord-Est, three merchants were operating in Havre-Saint-Pierre, and one in Port-la-Joye.

There were other businessmen in the colony, most notably the mill owners and the men referred to as "navigators." The latter owned boats and were often employed by the French authorities in Port-la-Joye to transport goods to places on the Island and to distant destinations such as Louisbourg, Quebec, Tatamagouche, and Baie Verte.

It was almost a century after the Deportation before Acadians became involved in commercial enterprises on Prince Edward Island. One of the factors that had hindered them was their status as tenant farmers. The large landowners retained the right for themselves or their associates to operate stores, taverns, and flour mills on their land grants.

The first Island Acadian to go into business was François (Frank) Arsenault who opened a store in Nail Pond around 1845. He traded his merchandise for farm produce and seafood from the farmers and fishermen in the Tignish area. Joseph B. Poirier, who opened his first store in Miscouche in 1857, was another Acadian pioneer in the world of commerce. Other Acadians followed in his footsteps, most notably members of his extended family who went into business in Miscouche, Abram-Village, Wellington, Tignish, and St. Louis.

Jean-Pierre Roma in Trois-Rivières

Jean-Pierre Roma is the best known of the businessmen on Île Saint-Jean. He came from France and arrived in Trois-Rivières (present-day Brudenell Point) in 1732 as the administrator of the Compagnie de l'Est de l'Île Saint-Jean, of which he was one of the four shareholders. He planned to use Trois-Rivières not only as a fishing community, but also as a centre for trade between France, New France, and the West Indies.

Jean-Pierre Roma had an impressive amount of work done in Trois-Rivières. He had the cape levelled, two wharves constructed, a large area of land cleared, and had five houses, a depot, a bakery, a forge, and a stable built. He also had wells dug and an ice house constructed. Vegetable crops, wheat, and peas were stored in a huge cellar. He had many small boats built, along with two cisterns for water. Roma also had several roads opened in order to travel overland to Port-la-Joye and Havre-Saint-Pierre. At the latter location, he built cod-drying racks and cabins for the 55 fishermen who worked for his company.

Jean-Pierre Roma's company, which had faced numerous setbacks, collapsed in 1745 when his establishment was burned by British troops during the war between France and Great Britain. Roma left Île Saint-Jean the following year with the hope of coming back and rebuilding in Trois-Rivières. Unfortunately he was not able to fulfil his dream and never returned to the Island.

Reconstruction of a building from the Jean-Pierre Roma settlement. (Photo: Georges Arsenault)

The Miscouche merchant Gilbert DesRoches (1848-1915) standing in the doorway of his store. (Acadian Museum of P.E.I. Collection)

Thanks to their enterprising spirit and ambition, these early Acadian businessmen played an important role in the economy by creating jobs in their own communities, buying and exporting local produce, and granting credit.

Although there were many Acadian tradesmen such as carpenters, plumbers, mechanics, and painters, very few of them actually owned their own businesses. In the 1960s and 1970s, however, a number of Acadians did become entrepreneurs. Notable examples are Johnny Perry of Tignish, who established Perry's Construction Company in 1960, and Edmond and Simon Arsenault, who founded Northumberland Construction Ltd. in 1965 with its head office in Abram-Village. The latter company became a big employer in the Evangeline Region. After gaining experience with Northumberland Construction, a number of employees left to create their own small businesses in the building sector or related fields.

Especially since the 1980s, an increasing number of Acadians and francophones have started small and medium-sized businesses. In fact, entrepreneurship has been encouraged and supported by various organizations, including the Baie Acadienne Development Corporation; RDÉE Prince Edward Island Inc. (the provincial francophone economic development council); and the Acadian and Francophone Chamber of Commerce of P.E.I. which was established in 2002.

Dining room of Joseph J. Gaudet's Bunn's Café, Summerside, 1917. (Mildred Savidant Collection)

Acadians in Towns

In the second half of the 19th century, Acadian men and women started moving to Summerside, a small town that was experiencing growth thanks to the shipbuilding industry. According to the 1881 census, there were 2,853 inhabitants, 208 (or 7.2 per cent) of whom were of French ethnic origin. Most of them were Island-born Acadians. Thirty years later, the 1911 census indicated that there were 706 people of French origin, in other words, 26.4 per cent of the population.

Arsène (Archie) LeClair (1880-1971) was a cart driver in Summerside for 70 years. (MacNaught History Centre and Archives)

At that time, the vast majority of Acadians living in Summerside were working-class. There were numerous cart drivers, sailors, fishermen, and general labourers. There were also a few specialized tradesmen, such as carpenters, coopers, tinsmiths, and masons. Almost all the married Acadian women were housewives, although a few earned their living as laundresses or seamstresses. A number of young single women worked as maids in the homes of wealthy families, at the convent, or at the hospital. Very few Acadians managed to get more prestigious and better-paying jobs in the business sector.

The remarkable brothers Henry and Joseph J. Gaudet, both born in the 1880s, were among the first Acadian businessmen in their native town of Summerside. They were involved primarily in the entertainment and restaurant business. Around 1911, Henry Gaudet started making ice cream under the trademark Olympia and opened the Olympia Ice Cream Parlour that housed the Olympia Cabaret, a very popular dance hall, which, by the late 1920s, was considered one of the best dance halls in the Maritimes. Henry Gaudet was also a talented hockey player

PERRY HOUSE

I have opened a new Hotel on Queen Street, next door to the old Bank of Nova Scotia building, where I will be pleased to meet all my old patrons and many new ones.

The house has been thoroughly fitted up, and furnished in first-class style, and it is one of the most comfortable and convenient hotels in town for either permanent or transient boarders.

The terms are very reasonable and the accommodation all that can be desired.

Give me a call.

FRANK PERRY

L'Impartial, January 13, 1898.

whose love of sports led him to becoming the owner of the Crystal Rink. After starting out as a cart driver, his brother, Joseph J., nicknamed Joe Bunn, went into the restaurant business. Then in 1911, Joe, his brother Henry, and Roy Silliphant opened Happyland, one of the first movie theatres in Summerside. Joe Bunn eventually became the sole owner and in 1922 opened the Capitol Theatre that entertained moviegoers until the year 2000.

In contrast to the Catholic citizens of French ethnic origin in Summerside, the ones in Charlottetown took much longer to make their presence felt. First of all, there were fewer of them because the provincial capital was located farther away from most of the Acadian villages. According to the 1881 census of Charlottetown, there were 121 Catholics of French origin out of a total population of 11,485. However, this "French" population was more diversified to the extent that a number of these people were born in Nova Scotia, New Brunswick, and Quebec. Many of the families had one parent who was not of French origin. By 1911 there were 573 Catholics of French origin, which only represented 5.1 per cent of the total population of 11,203.

Chapter 5

The Catholic Church and Religious Life

Île Saint-Jean was colonized when Roman Catholicism was the state religion of France; consequently, the Catholic Church had considerable political power. When a colony was founded, the government made sure the Church played an active role.

When the Compagnie de l'Île Saint-Jean sent its first settlers from France to the Island in 1720, they were accompanied by two priests. Although these two missionaries only spent three years on the Island, they were quickly replaced. In fact, a succession of priests relayed each other on a fairly regular basis in Port-la-Joye and Havre-Saint-Pierre. Their work consisted of serving not only the settlers, but also the garrison and the colonial administrators in Port-la-Joye, as well as the Mi'kmaw population. They celebrated mass, took the sacraments to the settlers, gave religious instruction to the youth, and sometimes performed the duties of Notary and Justice of the Peace.

In the early 1720s, a church was built in Port-la-Joye and in Havre-Saint-Pierre, thus creating the first two parishes. With the arrival of a large number of Acadians after 1748, new parishes were founded with a resident priest in Malpec, Pointe-Prime, and Rivière-du-Nord-Est.

In the course of his inspection tour of the colony in 1751, the engineer Louis Franquet met most of the settlers. Everywhere he went in the newly settled areas they asked him to get them a priest. According to his report, the settlers were very "zealous for religion, even somewhat superstitious." The settlers needed priests to administer the main sacraments prescribed by the

Catholic Church—namely baptism, confession, communion, and marriage—and to prepare them for a "good death."

The Acadians who settled on the Island after the Deportation also requested the presence of a priest to fulfil their spiritual needs. The British Protestant merchants who recruited Acadians realized very quickly that if they wanted to attract and keep these workers, it was essential to find them a priest. The merchants' first step was to pressure the British colonial authorities to allow a Catholic clergyman into the colony. Then they asked the Bishop of Quebec to dispatch a priest whom they promised to maintain. Representatives of the small Acadian community also went to see the bishop but their requests were in vain because of the lack of priests throughout the huge diocese of Quebec after the Conquest of 1760. Consequently, for several years, the Acadians on the Island had to be content with brief visits from missionaries who were responsible for all the Acadians living the Gulf of St. Lawrence region. In the absence of a priest, a leader in the community would baptize children and hear marriage vows.

St. John the Baptist Church in Miscouche, built in 1822. (*Illustrated Historical Atlas of the Province of Prince Edward Island*, 1880, p. 159)

The first priests to settle on the Island under the British regime were Scottish: Father James MacDonald arrived in 1770, followed by Father Angus Bernard MacEachern in 1790. Having learned French, they could be of service to the Acadian population. Fathers Amable Pichard and Jacques-Ladislas-Joseph de Calonne, both from France, spent a few years each on the Island

The Ways that I Have Found

In the years following the Deportation, the Acadians on Île Saint-Jean asked Monsignor Jean-Olivier Briand, the bishop of Quebec, on several occasions to send them a priest. As his response of September 16, 1770, indicates (below, translated from French), this was no simple matter.

What now must you do in turn for your salvation and for your religion? Here are three steps that you can take. The first is to write to the Governor of Halifax requesting that he send you Mr. Bailly, missionary, or to fetch him yourselves. Here is the second step: Father de la Brosse has to travel to Chaleur Bay; you must go find him there or ask the Governor of Halifax to give you written permission to go find him so you can take him to your island.

If you cannot undertake that, I have just spoken to a priest who promised me that if next Spring you send a suitable small boat, that is to say a small schooner or a good decked-over shallop, he would spend two months with you in order to instruct you, hear confessions, give communion, baptize children, supplement baptismal ceremonies, reconcile and rehabilitate marriages, and marry those who come forth. My Dear Children, those are the ways I have found; the latter would be the most costly for you, but if the two others are not successful, you should not hesitate to take it. One must sacrifice everything for salvation.

Msgr. Jean-Olivier Briand, bishop of the Diocese of Quebec from 1766 to 1784. (Archives nationales de Québec, Collection Initiale)

Many of your young people have not seen the celebration of the Holy Sacrifice of the Mass, have not confessed, have not received the Blessed Sacrament of the Eucharist, and consequently know their religion only through ideas and words. That is very little, too little in fact, to instil in them invincible ties to the religion that we observe with so much admiration and satisfaction in the old Acadians.

between 1799 and 1804, relieving Father MacEachern's burden. They were followed by two priests from Quebec: Jean-Louis Beaubien arrived in 1812 and was replaced by Joseph-Étienne Cécile in 1818. Although they resided in Rustico, they were called upon to serve all the Acadians and Mi'kmaq in the colony, along with the inhabitants of the Magdalen Islands.

Given the vast territory, the priest could only visit each mission two or three times a year and stayed for just two weeks. Under these circumstances, laymen were forced to play an important role. They performed various duties normally reserved for the clergy. Thus on Sundays and religious holidays, people would go to church to hear "White Mass" and Vespers. There was no consecration and the most literate and respected men in the community presided over the reading of the prayers of the Mass.

In 1828, Sylvain-Éphrem Perrey (Poirier) from Tignish became the first Island-born Acadian to be ordained to the priesthood. For many years, he was responsible for all the Acadian parishes in Prince County. Little by little, the number of priests increased. Most of the ones assigned to Acadian parishes were Scots born on the Island and Canadians (in other words, from Quebec). It was not until 1884 that a second Islander, François-Xavier Gallant from Rustico, was received into the priesthood.

Rev. Sylvain-Éphrem Perrey (1802-1887). First Acadian from P.E.I. to be ordained to the priesthood. (P.E.I. Acadian Research Centre, 1.357)

Under the Leadership of the Clergy

By the 1860s most of the Acadian parishes had a resident priest. The parish priest's activities went far beyond strictly religious matters. He played a role in education, cultural development, agriculture, social activities, and the creation of new settlements. Benefiting from a special status, the priest had enormous powers. Before undertaking any project that might affect community life, parishioners first made sure they had the priest's support, otherwise nothing could be done. In an article published on June 1, 1868 in the *Summerside Progress*, an Acadian wrote: "The Acadians are peaceable in character, and strongly attached to the religion of their forefathers—which is the Roman Catholic. They have great reverence for their clergy, in whom they place an almost unbounded confidence."

Once a resident priest arrived, both the religious and secular aspects of parish life took on a new life. Thanks to the priest's initiative and his parishioners' support, new churches, convents, and schools were built, libraries established, and numerous organizations created to further the development of the community.

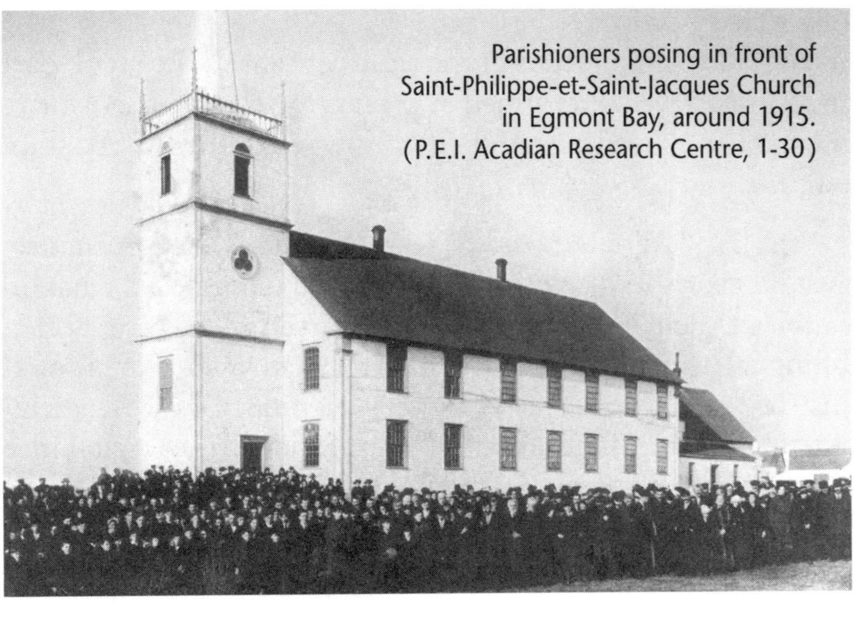

Parishioners posing in front of Saint-Philippe-et-Saint-Jacques Church in Egmont Bay, around 1915. (P.E.I. Acadian Research Centre, 1-30)

Of all the accomplishments, Georges-Antoine Belcourt's were without question the most impressive. This enterprising priest, who served in Rustico from 1859 to 1869, contributed substantially to the socioeconomic revival of his parishioners. The repercussions of his work were felt throughout the Acadian community on the Island. He established the Catholic Institute of Rustico, a temperance society that served as a springboard for his other achievements such as the Farmers' Bank of Rustico (the precursor of credit unions in Canada), a secondary school for training bilingual teachers, a brass band, a library, and a settlement project.

Rev. Georges-Antoine Belcourt, parish priest of Rustico from 1859 to 1869. (Public Archives and Records Office of P.E.I.)

Like Father Belcourt, the French-speaking members of the clergy proved to be the most staunch supporters of the Acadian cause. They took part in all the movements aimed at promoting the social advancement of the Acadians and the preservation of the Acadian culture.

English-language priests who served in predominantly Acadian parishes also devoted themselves to the social rehabilitation of their Acadian parishioners. Even if they were often bilingual, these priests saw no particular advantage in promoting the French language, which they felt hindered the Acadians' integration into Island society dominated by the anglophone majority. The anglicizing mentality of some members of the

English-language clergy was especially apparent in the 1920s. Parishes with a high proportion of francophone worshippers were given to priests who hardly spoke any French. Some of them were even opposed to the use of French in the religious life of the parish. This attitude obviously hampered efforts to promote and preserve the French language and the Acadian identity.

The Acadian community was concerned about the lack of French-speaking priests in the regions where most of the Acadian and francophone population lived. The issue was raised with the bishop on four occasions between 1946 and 1965. The Acadians drew his attention to the lack of religious services in French, unilingual English-language priests put in charge of Acadian parishes, Acadian priests placed in parishes that were entirely anglophone, and the virtual absence of Acadians in the ecclesiastical hierarchy.

Corpus Christi procession in Miscouche, around 1960.
(Elva Arsenault Collection)

By the end of the 1960s, the French language was finally given a more prominent position in the diocese. Not only did some parishes receive Acadian priests for the first time in 50 years, but a number of diocesan services were offered in French.

While parish priests played an important role in the Acadians' religious and secular life, and their spectacular churches were visible proof of their attachment to the Catholic faith, their religious expression went far beyond those spheres. For a long time, religion also meant a way of life imbued with traditional rituals and beliefs, institutionalized ceremonies, and strict rules prescribed by the Church.

Important transformations began to take place in the 1960s, especially as a result of the Second Vatican Council that defined a new orientation for the Roman Catholic Church in the modern world. Innumerable changes were made that affected almost every aspect of the religious life of Catholics. For instance, the ceremonies of worship were changed to facilitate better communication with the faithful; the Church became less authoritarian and stressed the participation of lay people; and a religion of fear and authority gave way to a religion of trust and love.

Rev. Nazaire Poirier presiding at the blessing of the fishing boats in Egmont Bay, around 1958. (Elva Arsenault Collection)

Island Acadians, like Catholics elsewhere, experienced radical changes in religious practices and observances. This upheaval resulted not only from the Second Vatican

Council, but also from the vast sociocultural transformations that began in the 1960s. Many people stopped going to Mass regularly and no longer observed certain forms of worship. Civil and mixed marriages became more frequent, with birth control families became smaller, and religious vocations dwindled.

First communion at the Notre-Dame-du-Mont-Carmel Church in 1950. (Marguerite and Robert Gallant Collection)

Today, the Catholic religion occupies an important place in the life of many Acadians on the Island, but it no longer has the influence and significance that it had before the 1960s. In the past, if one called oneself Acadian, one had to be a practising Catholic. That is no longer the case today. Many Acadians who proclaim their Acadian identity no longer observe Catholic religious practices and a number belong to other religions.

Daughters of Agape Gaudet and Judith Bernard of Tignish, who were among the many Acadian women who entered religious life by joining the Congregation of Notre-Dame de Montréal. (J. Henri Gaudet fonds, P.E.I. Acadian Research Centre)

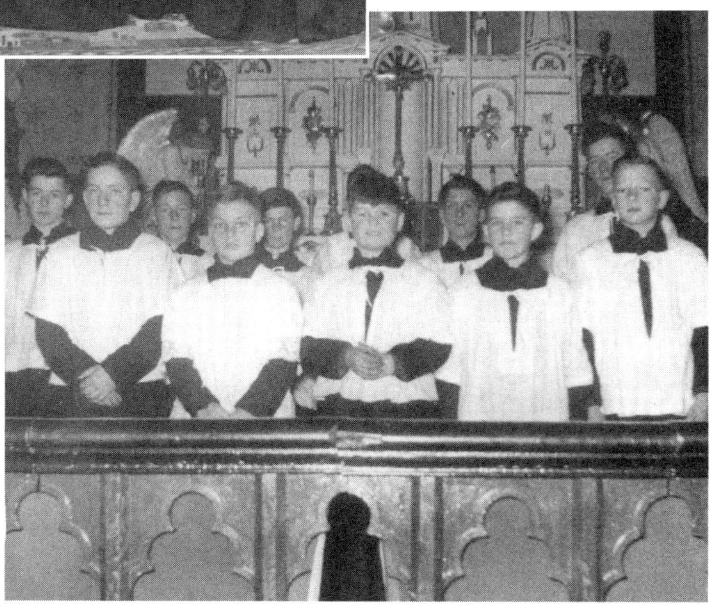

St. Augustine Parish altar boys in Rustico, around 1955. (Yvonne Doucette Collection)

Religious Practices and Beliefs in Bygone Days

During storms, to protect the household from thunder, the windows of the house were sprinkled with holy water.

†

When changing your underwear, you had to cross yourself to ward off evil thoughts.

†

To discourage people from entering dance halls, priests said that guardian angels stayed outside by the door and never went inside.

†

Girls should not whistle because it would make the Blessed Virgin cry.

†

You should never plough the ground on All Souls' Day (November 2) because you might hurt the dead who come back to earth that day.

†

During Lent, you gave up candy and sweets, and many men gave up cigarettes and alcohol.

◆

Palmer Road's Immaculate Conception Church designed by Montreal architect Édouard Meloche and built in 1892. (Photo: Georges Arsenault)

Chapter 6

Education

Formal education in Acadian communities on Prince Edward Island only became available in the early 1800s. During the French regime, a few settlers could read and write, but the majority were illiterate. This was not an unusual phenomenon for the period since only a small percentage of the populations of Europe and the colonies in North America had the possibility of acquiring an education.

In the 50 years that followed the Deportation, the clergy were generally the only people who provided any education for Acadians on the Island. They ensured a minimum of instruction, concentrating for the most part on religious teachings.

The first Acadian school opened in 1815 in Rustico, thanks to the initiative of the missionary Jean-Louis Beaubien. In the absence of a teacher, he placed the young Acadian François Buote, to whom he had given a rudimentary education, in charge of the school. The following year, Dominique Charles Auffray, a Frenchman from Brittany, settled in Tignish and taught classes in the area. In 1817, Louis Séniat, another Frenchman, opened a school in Rollo Bay.

Despite the efforts of a few individuals, the majority of Acadians remained illiterate for a long time. John McGregor, a former member of the Legislative Assembly, wrote around 1830 that Acadians had virtually no schooling. He also stated that most of the men understood English but that in his opinion French would remain their mother tongue for many years.

François Buote, the First Acadian Teacher on the Island

Born in Rustico around 1794, François Buote was the son of France (François) Buote and Marie Belliveau. As a young boy he was invited by Father Jean-Louis Beaubien to live in the presbytery. The priest gave him a rudimentary education in the hopes that he would pursue studies for the priesthood, but François Buote decided instead to become a teacher. In a letter written to Monsignor Joseph-Octave Plessis, bishop of Quebec, on November 15, 1814, Father Beaubien stated that he was planning to open a school in Rustico:

> *I believe that a sure way of bringing up young people in piety is to educate them as much as possible. That is why I am going to undertake to have a school built and, since I do not have a schoolmaster such as I would like, I shall use my boy who can read quite well, who is starting to write and is doing his tables; thereafter I shall do my best to keep an eye on the school myself.*

That is how François Buote became the first Acadian teacher on the Island in 1815. Around 1822, he moved to Miscouche to teach, and then, in 1834, to Tignish where he taught until 1857.

Since he spoke English fluently, his compatriots often called upon him to conduct their business. In 1847, François Buote was the first Acadian to be appointed Commissioner of the Small Claims Court.

François Buote married Victoire Gaudet from Rustico. They had nine children, including a son called Gilbert who, following in his father's footsteps, became a teacher. In 1893, Gilbert and his son François-Joseph, a printer, founded *L'Impartial* in Tignish: the first French-language newspaper on Prince Edward Island.

François Buote died in St. Felix, in the parish of Tignish, on November 30, 1873, at the age of 79.

Until 1825, the schools that existed on the Island operated without any financial support from the government. It was in that year that the Legislative Assembly voted for funds designed to encourage the establishment of public schools. In subsequent years, the few schoolmasters who were teaching in Acadian communities received a salary from the colonial government. In 1831, the government even voted the sum of £36 be given to "worthy" teachers in Acadian schools, stipulating that no one teacher could receive more than £6. That was less than the amount granted to teachers in the English-speaking districts of the colony. Government authorities felt that teachers in the Acadian schools and the schools themselves were inferior because classes were given almost entirely in French. However, if a French-speaking teacher obtained his First Class teacher's certificate from the Board of Education—in other words, his qualifications to teach in English—he would receive the same salary as English-speaking teachers.

As francophone teachers gradually became more proficient in English, they started teaching a bit of English in Acadian schools. In 1846, the school inspector reported that Acadians were gradually taking advantage of an education in English. The following year, he wrote in his annual report that English Reading was now part of the curriculum in almost all the Acadian schools, which, in his opinion, made that category of school more useful.

Amendments to the Education Act resulted in an increase in the quantity of English taught in Acadian schools. In 1854, a modification to the Education Act forced Acadian teachers to teach Reading, Writing, and Arithmetic in English, otherwise they would lose the salary the government paid them.

From 1847 until 1863, when the Board of Education abolished the category of "Acadian teachers," the Catholic clergy were responsible for certifying prospective teachers and especially for attesting to the teacher's aptitude to teach in

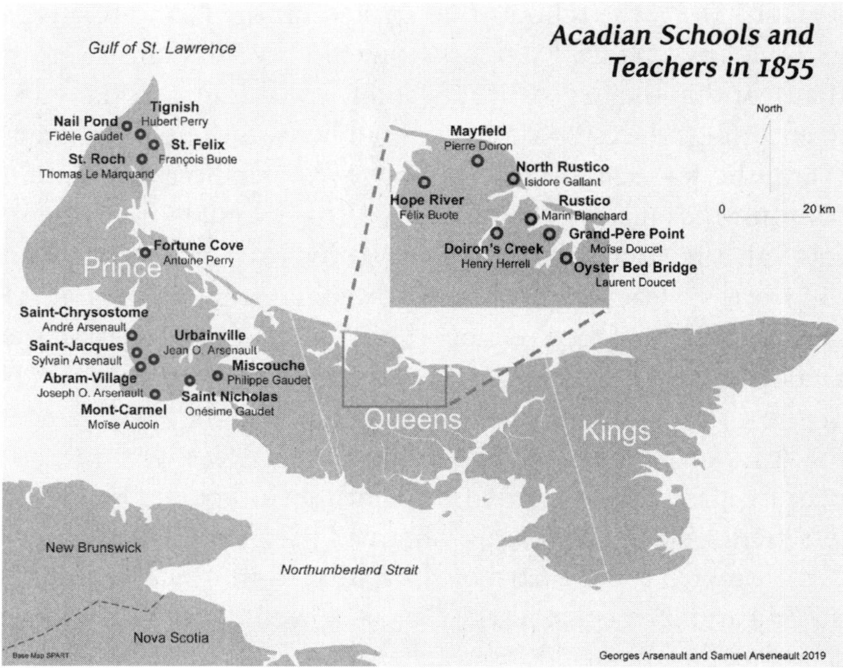

French. After 1863, in order to obtain their teacher's certificate, Acadians had to attend the Normal School in Charlottetown where all the examinations were given in English. There was no longer any question of demonstrating one's ability in the French language. In theory that marked the end of French-language schools on Prince Edward Island, but, in fact, a great deal of French continued to be taught in most of the Acadian schools, especially in the lower grades.

The Education Act of 1877 stated that public schools had to be nondenominational and that only prescribed textbooks could be used. This had a major impact on Acadian schools because it meant that most of the French books were removed since they were deemed to be too imbued with religious principles. However, the law left unresolved the whole issue of French-language education. Henceforth, Acadian pupils would learn to read using the *Royal Readers*, a series of bilingual readers from Nova Scotia.

Sisters of the Congregation of Notre Dame and their students at the Tignish Convent around 1890. (J. Henri Gaudet, *Photo Historica, P.E.I., Tignish Î.-P.-É., 1899-1999*, p. 121)

Miscouche Convent, around 1880. The Sisters of the Congregation of Notre Dame moved into the building in 1864. (P.E.I. Acadian Research Centre, 44.83)

A Revitalization

The anglicization of Acadian schools was a subject of discussion among the delegates attending the second Acadian National Convention that was held in Miscouche in 1884. They passed a motion that included the following demands: that the standard of the teaching of French in Acadian school districts be the same as the standard of the teaching of English; that Acadian teachers teaching French receive the same salary as other teachers; and that the inspection of Acadian schools be done in French.

Thanks to the pressure of a few community leaders, the Board of Education implemented a number of measures designed to improve the quality of teaching in Acadian schools. In 1890, Joseph-Octave Arsenault (not to be confused with the politician of the same name) was hired as French professor at Prince of Wales College (to which was affiliated the provincial Normal School) and as principal of the Model School where future teachers did their practice teaching. In 1892, while still keeping those positions, he became the first francophone school inspector of Acadian schools.

Joseph-Octave Arsenault (1866-1918), first Acadian School Inspector in P.E.I. (Georges Arsenault Collection)

The Acadian Teachers' Association of Prince Edward Island was established in 1893 to encourage the teaching of French in the public schools attended by Acadian children. The association held annual conventions until 1972 and played an important role in the promotion of the French language and the Acadian identity. The most significant accomplishments of the association include the creation of "regional assemblies"—precursors of parent-teacher meetings (1894)—the founding of the Saint Thomas Aquinas Society (1919), the organization of French competitions (1930), and the establishment of the Acadian Historical Society of Prince Edward Island (1955).

Despite these accomplishments, the situation of French-language education on Prince Edward Island remained problematic for a long time. In most cases, the quality of the teaching depended entirely on the efforts and initiatives of individual teachers who wanted to improve the way their mother

To Make a Point of Raising This Important Matter

The following is the translation of part of a letter that an Acadian published in the newspaper *Le Moniteur acadien* on December 20, 1884. He deplores the state of the teaching of French in Acadian schools. The vast majority of teachers at the time were men.

> *The lack of French instruction in our schools is a major shortcoming that I notice in Prince Edward Island. Is it the government or the teachers' fault? Both, I think, because if the government paid more attention to the education of our young men in the French language as well as the English language, our towns and countryside would be inhabited by better citizens...*
>
> *The introduction of French grammar in our schools would be a good thing for our children; but to introduce it, we would have to have teachers capable of teaching it; proof that it is absolutely essential for us to have a French Department at the Normal School where our young men going into a career in teaching could receive a good education in French. Our public figures should have realized that a long time ago and should have made a point of raising this important matter.*

tongue was taught. The lack of francophone teachers also meant that school districts were often forced to hire teachers who spoke only English. In 1926, for example, of the 63 teachers responsible for Acadian classrooms, 17 (thus, more than 25 per cent) of them were anglophones. In the majority of Acadian schools, the French curriculum was limited to Reading,

Students at St. Edward School in 1926. (Lorraine LeBlanc Collection)

Acadian Teachers' Annual Conventions

From 1894 to 1972, the Acadian Teachers' Association of Prince Edward Island held an annual convention. It took place in a different parish every year and was attended by teachers along with priests from the Acadian parishes, Acadian public figures, and a large number of parents. The program included presentations on various topics given by teachers and other participants at the convention. The following were the subjects discussed at the 1916 convention:

- *Parents' duties to their children* – F.E. Doiron
- *Teachers' duties to their pupils* – Clothilde Arsenault
- *Teaching difficulties* – Denis D. Arsenault
- *Parent-teacher relations* – Marguerite LeClair
- *The situation of Acadians on P.E.I.* – J. Henri Blanchard
- *The art of reading well* – François Arsenault
- *How to study* – Pierre LeClair
- *Nature* – Jeanne Arsenault

Participants at the 6th annual convention of the Acadian Teachers' Association of Prince Edward Island held in Miscouche in 1898. Until the early 1900s, the majority of the teachers were men. (Acadian Museum of P.E.I. Collection)

Grammar, Dictation, and a small amount of Writing, taught by teachers who had all received their training in English. By the 1930s, half the Acadian schoolchildren, including the ones living in Summerside and Charlottetown, were attending entirely English-language schools.

French-language education started to improve in the 1960s, especially in the Evangeline Region where the population is the most homogeneous. The Evangeline Regional High School opened under the direction of the sisters of Notre-Dame-du-Sacré-Coeur, an Acadian religious congregation known for promoting the French language and Acadian culture. It was not long before most of the classes in the schools in the region were taught by teachers who had graduated from French-language postsecondary institutions. In 1972, when the government decided to consolidate all the small school boards into four large administrative units, the Evangeline School Unit, created in 1960, was left intact because of its special status. It became Unit 5, with French as the language of instruction and administration.

Evangeline Regional High School students and teaching staff at the opening of the school in 1960. (George Wotton Collection , P.E.I. Acadian Research Centre)

The reorganization of the school system affected the education of Acadians living in other regions differently because their schools were located in the four large anglophone administrative units. Gradually, as small schools closed, students went to consolidated schools where the only French curriculum was French as a second language, which did not start until Grade Three or sometimes Grade Seven.

Major transformations took place in the field of education throughout Canada in the 1970s. In the aftermath of the *Official Languages Act,* passed in 1969 by the federal government, Canadians gradually become more aware of the importance of knowing the country's both official languages. The federal government made funds available for the provinces so they could improve French-language education for francophones in a minority situation and for anglophones who wanted to enrol their children in French Immersion. The Saint Thomas Aquinas Society (Société Saint-Thomas-d'Aquin or SSTA) urged the Department of Education to take advantage of these funding programs. As a result, a coordinator of French-language education was created in each of the five administrative units in the province. A French Immersion program was introduced in a number of schools, including ones attended by many Acadian children.

The SSTA, the primary group that speaks on behalf of the Acadian and francophone community on the Island, began a promotional campaign for the establishment of French-language schools outside the Evangeline Region. On the one hand, parents were encouraged to advocate for French-language education for their children, and, on the other, pressure was put on the provincial government to amend the Education Act to make education available in French where it was requested. As a result of the transfer of the federal Department of Veterans Affairs from Ottawa to Charlottetown, the first French-language school was opened in Charlottetown in 1980 and was eventually given the name École François-Buote.

Francis C. Blanchard and Roxanne Parent at the Charlottetown French school in 1981 with the students from Grades 2 to 8. The school opened in September 1980 with five students. It was officially named École François-Buote in 1982. (Photo: *La Voix acadienne*)

Starting in 1988, before other French schools were constructed, francophone parents were forced to go to court in order to obtain the right to manage their own schools. A province-wide francophone school board was then created in 1990. Litigation before the Supreme Court of Canada in the year 2000 was also necessary in order to confirm the parents' right to have their children educated in French "in their community." Following these hard-won battles, the Acadian community celebrated the opening of French schools in Summerside, Rustico, West Prince, and Eastern Kings.

On January 10, 2000, the Supreme Court of Canada sided with two parents in Summerside who demanded a French school for their community. L. to r.: Madeleine Costa, lawyer Robert MacConnell, Noëlla Arsenault and Colleen Soltermann, President of the Fédération des parents de l'Î.-P.-É. (La Belle-Alliance Ltd. Collection)

Thus, French schools opened in regions of the province where for many generations children had not had access to education in French. Many parents who never had the opportunity to learn French can now take advantage of these schools to give back their ancestral language to their children.

The Island Community College

In 1993, the Société Saint-Thomas-d'Aquin created the Société éducative de l'Île-du-Prince-Édouard (the Education Society of P.E.I.) with the aim of offering continuing education in French for adults. The Centre de formation aux adultes was opened in Wellington and the following year a partnership was established with the Collège de l'Acadie in Nova Scotia in order to provide community-college-level training courses on the Island. The partnership came to an end in 2006.

In 2008, the training centre became the Collège de l'Île, a French-language community college with satellite campuses in Wellington, Charlottetown, and Deblois.

The Island's first French-language post-secondary graduation at the Collège de l'Acadie in Wellington in 1996. (Photo: *La Voix acadienne*)

Chapter 7

Living in French

In 1860 there were about 9,000 Acadians living on Prince Edward Island. That is an estimate because prior to the Island joining Confederation in 1873, the censuses carried out in the colony did not indicate the inhabitants' ethnic origin or their mother tongue. In the spring of 1861, when the Legislative Assembly voted on a Bill pertaining to the census planned for that year, Stanislaus F. Perry, the only Acadian member of the Legislature, introduced a motion that a special column be added to the census takers' document so they could record the number of French Acadians in each family. His motion was defeated. Among the opponents was Colonel George Hamilton Gray, future Father of Confederation. In his opinion, there was no need to make this kind of distinction because, as a people, Islanders should aim "to become amalgamated rather than keep up unnecessary distinctions."

Stanislas F. Perry (1823-1898) from Tignish. Elected in 1854, he was the first Acadian member of the P.E.I. Legislative Assembly and in 1874 was the first Acadian from the Maritime provinces to sit in the House of Commons. (Brian Doucette Collection)

The election of Tignish native Stanislaus F. Perry (Poirier) to the Legislative Assembly in 1854 was a sign that the Acadian community on the Island was beginning to emerge from isolation and becoming more open towards the English-speaking population. A number of well-educated men, strongly influenced by the Catholic clergy, formed a small but significant elite.

The leaders of this new generation no longer accepted that the Acadian people go their own way and remain a disadvantaged group. They made it their mission to see that Acadians were on an equal footing with English-speaking inhabitants of the Island in the social, economic, and political spheres. They were well aware, however, that it would take time before that could happen. In 1868, an Acadian of the new generation wrote a long article in English in the *Summerside Progress* in which he delivered a vibrant plea for his compatriots to change their attitudes and abandon some of their old customs. According to the author of the article, Island Acadians were still a separate people:

> Although British subjects, the Acadians in the Island are in reality a separate people, holding themselves aloof, in most of the social affairs of life, from their fellow-colonists who speak a different language from their own, and who are too often apt to look upon them as an ignorant and antiquated class of people. The Acadians, on the other hand, while they look upon their more conceited fellow-colonists as their superiors in learning and wealth, are repelled from proper sympathy with them by the remembrance of the sufferings their fathers endured at the time of the conquest of these Provinces by the English, and subsequently.

The changes advocated by the Acadian men of the new generation caused concern among a certain segment of the population. These men knew that any revival meant breaking down the cultural isolation that had been nurtured by previous generations. How could they convince their compatriots to come out of their isolation and develop in the dominant English-speaking society without losing their own language and culture? Some maintained that a certain degree of anglicization was necessary in order for the Acadian people to catch up to the rest of the Island population. Others, while not opposed to learning English as a tool for social advancement, were firmly committed to keeping their French language and culture intact.

Unifying the Acadian People

Important changes were taking place in the Acadian community, not only in Prince Edward Island but also in New Brunswick and Nova Scotia. Between 1881 and 1890, Island Acadians joined their compatriots from the other Maritime provinces at three conventions to discuss issues related to their socioeconomic and linguistic status and to take steps to unite the

Raising of the first Acadian flag on August 16, 1884, in Miscouche. The flag was officially adopted the previous day during the second National Acadian Convention. Painting by Claude Picard. (Acadian Museum of P.E.I. Collection)

Acadian people. These conventions were held in Memramcook (1881), Miscouche (1884), and Church Point (1890). At the first two conventions, the delegates, representing a unified Acadie, adopted a national feast day (Our Lady of the Assumption, celebrated on August 15), a flag (the French tricolour flag with a yellow star in the blue stripe), an anthem (*Ave Maris Stella*), and a motto (*l'Union fait la force*, Strength in Unity).

Thanks in part to the accessibility of trains, a considerable number of Island Acadians attended these conventions. At the one in Miscouche, the delegates discussed at great length the problem of anglicization and several of the most important resolutions adopted were related to the French language and education in French on the Island.

In the years that followed these impressive gatherings, the Acadian community on the Island benefited from a number of initiatives designed, for the most part, to preserve and promote life in French. In addition to improvements in the area of French-language education introduced in the early 1890s, the most important accomplishment was definitely the creation of the French-language newspaper *L'Impartial*. This weekly, founded in Tignish in 1893 by schoolteacher Gilbert Buote and his son François-Joseph, took on the role of championing the Acadian cause. During the 20-odd years of its existence, *L'Impartial* served

L'IMPARTIAL
L'Union fait la Force
LA CIE. DE PUB. DE L'IMPARTIAL, PROPRIETAIRE. G. BUOTE, RÉDACTEUR. F. J. BUOTE, GÉRANT
VOL. 4. NO. 7 TIGNISH, ILE du PRINCE EDOUARD, JEUDI LE 21 AVRIL 1904. II ANNEE

as the voice of the Acadian nationalist discourse and encouraged Acadians to support their patriotic and nationalist associations and above all to equip themselves with institutions that could enhance the development of their community.

Strength in Unity

The following is the translation of an extract from the first editorial in the weekly newspaper *L'Impartial*, published on June 22, 1893. Using as its motto *L'Union fait la force* (Strength in Unity), the newspaper declared that it aimed "To advance the Acadian cause in social, intellectual, and moral domains."

> *Today, for the first time in the annals of Prince Edward Island, a French-language newspaper is sending its greetings to the Acadian families of our province. It is a long-awaited, sincere, and devoted friend that is coming to take its place in our homes in order to entertain us and to relate to us that which, until now, we were forced to learn through newspapers written in a foreign language.*
>
> *Sometimes it is said that the Acadian people are somewhat apathetic about reading and instruction in general. We believe we are expressing the feelings of our compatriots in repudiating this false and erroneous assertion. If the Acadians of our province have not always given French education the attention it deserved, it is because adverse circumstances prevented them from doing so.*
>
> *Subjected to a regime that took no account of our nationality, we were forced to study and learn the English language in order to keep abreast of the affairs of the country we live in, and it should also be said that we have mastered that foreign language in a way that has surprised even the English themselves. However, let us be frank, the progress we have made in those efforts has almost led us to completely forget the language our forefathers bequeathed to us.*

The educator Gilbert Buote (1833-1904), from Tignish, founded the weekly *L'Impartial* in 1893 to defend the interests of Acadians and to promote the French language. (*L'Impartial Illustré*, 1899, p. 60)

Starting in 1905, the establishment of branches of the Société mutuelle l'Assomption on the Island marked another important step in the advancement of the Acadian cause. Founded in 1903 by Acadians in Massachusetts, this mutual society spread to almost every parish where there was a sizeable group of Acadians. Its goals were to promote the social, intellectual, and moral well-being of the Acadians; to oversee an insurance fund for the protection of their families; and to set up an educational fund to finance the formation of an elite. Members met regularly at the local level until the 1960s when the branches were dissolved. On several occasions the *Assomptionnistes*, as they were called, met for provincial conventions to take stock of their accomplishments and the challenges facing the Acadian community.

The Saint Thomas Aquinas Society (Société Saint-Thomas-d'Aquin or SSTA), another important organization, was formed at the 1919 annual convention of the Acadian Teachers' Association of Prince Edward Island. Although the immediate task of the SSTA was to raise funds for the education of youth, the overall goal was the development of French and Acadian

Participants at the 1951 summer camp organized by the Acadian Students Association of P.E.I. The association brought together young Islanders, most of whom were sponsored by the Saint Thomas Aquinas Society to study at various French-language colleges in Quebec and the Maritimes. (Georges Arsenault Collection)

We Must Act as Speedily as Possible

The following is part of the speech given in French in 1937 by Professor J. Henri Blanchard, Secretary-Treasurer of the SSTA, at the second Convention on the French language in Canada that was held in Quebec City. He describes the status of French life on the Island province and launches an appeal for help.

> *First of all, the vast majority of our 14,000 Acadians live in the countryside; they are almost all farmers or fishermen. Very few of them have any secondary schooling.* [...] *The number of Acadians on the Island who have received some sort of training at college is ridiculously small.*
>
> [We suffer from] *an extreme shortage of chiefs and leaders with all the consequences that entails. If we had those indispensable leaders now, it would not be too late to stem the massive tides that continuously threaten to engulf us.*
>
> *We do, of course, have the Saint Thomas Aquinas Society that collects some monies to pay for the higher education of two students. But this is so little, given the dangers that threaten us from all sides. If we wish to train the indispensable leaders without whom we, as a French-language group, shall surely disappear, then we must act as speedily as possible; otherwise it will be too late.*

Professor J. Henri Blanchard (1881-1968), a founding member of the Saint Thomas Aquinas Society in 1919 and its main pillar and inspiration for many years. (Georges Arsenault Collection)

life in the province. By the 1950s there were about 30 local branches of the SSTA, which were responsible primarily for collecting funds and recruiting members.

With support from a number of postsecondary institutions in Quebec, New Brunswick, and Nova Scotia, the SSTA was able to grant scholarships and loans to numerous young Acadian men and women who wanted to further their education. To encourage reading in French, subsidies were also given to Acadian schools so they could purchase French-language books for their libraries. After 1944, while intensifying its efforts to ensure the preservation of French and the promotion of Acadian culture, the SSTA gradually became the main organization to speak on behalf of the Acadian community on the Island.

Judge Aubin E. Arsenault (1870-1968), son of Senator Joseph-Octave Arsenault, was prime minister of P.E.I. from 1917 to 1919. He was the first Acadian to become premier of a Canadian province. He sat on the Supreme Court of P.E.I. from 1921 to 1946. (P.E.I. Acadian Research Centre, 32-71)

Against All Odds

The anglicization and acculturation of Island Acadians, which had begun in the mid-1800s, became increasingly widespread. According to the 1951 Canadian census, for example, 42 per cent of the 15,477 Islanders of French ethnic origin no longer considered French their mother tongue. That percentage continued to grow, as subsequent censuses showed.

This ever-increasing assimilation was caused by a number of factors. In many schools French was poorly taught, if at all. For decades several Acadian parishes only had English-speaking priests, some of whom sought openly to anglicize their Acadian parishioners. The arrival of television in the 1950s meant that a substantial amount of English entered people's homes. To find work, more and more Acadians moved to the English-speaking towns of Summerside and Charlottetown, which some described as the "graveyards of French life." And, last but not least, marriages between francophones and anglophones were more common and, as in other cultures, the children adopted the dominant language.

It should also be stressed that the minority status of the French language on the Island and elsewhere in Canada did not facilitate its retention. French was often looked down upon. In parishes and areas with a homogeneous Acadian population, French remained the language for public meetings, religious services, and even for work. However, in ethnically mixed parishes, where Acadians were still in the majority, the English language dominated most of the time in public spheres, whether it was at church, at school, in the workplace, or in community organizations. French was thus reduced to the language spoken with friends and in the privacy of one's home. Given those circumstances, it is understandable why many Acadians felt a sense of inferiority with regard to French and even more so with regard to Acadian French which is often scorned. It is not surprising that some Acadians associated their socioeconomic inferiority with their Acadian identity and the way they spoke. To avoid being stigmatized, they chose assimilation as a strategy for social advancement.

Substantial help arrived from Ottawa after the *Official Languages Act* was passed by the Parliament of Canada in 1969. This law had major repercussions throughout the country. At last a favourable climate was created for French Canadians, especially francophones in a minority situation whose linguistic and cultural survival was in jeopardy.

The federal government implemented programs designed to develop bilingualism in Canada. These programs affected the federal civil service, arts and culture, school instruction in the official languages, and the official language minority communities. One of these programs in particular was aimed at providing these communities with the necessary tools for their development.

In the case of Prince Edward Island, the federal government recognized the SSTA as the official voice for the francophone community and the organization with which the government would collaborate to implement its program for sociocultural action. The SSTA, which had operated on a strictly volunteer basis, thus received grants that enabled it to hire staff for the development and expansion of its activities. This unprecedented support on the part of the government sparked a long-awaited

The 1998 annual meeting of the Saint Thomas Aquinas Society chaired by its president Antoine Richard. Hired in 1969 as socio-cultural development officer, he became the society's first paid employee. (Photo: Georges Arsenault)

revival. An impressive amount of work was done to raise awareness and organize activities in all the Acadian areas. A number of organizations were created to validate and revitalize the French language and Acadian culture in the province. The SSTA also demanded that the provincial government commit to the development of Acadian communities by offering government services in French and especially by improving access to French-language education.

The SSTA also ensured that Island francophones had access to media in their own language. After 60 years without a French-language newspaper, in 1976 the SSTA founded the weekly *La Voix acadienne* and lobbied CBC/Radio-Canada for the extension of French-language services to the entire province.

Launch of the weekly newspaper *La Voix acadienne* on June 16, 1976. Standing, from left, Jean Doiron, editor; Claudette Maddix, publicist; Léonce Bernard, MLA; Pierre Arsenault, president of the Saint Thomas Aquinas Society. Seated, Claudette Arsenault, secretary. (Photo: *La Voix acadienne*)

The SSTA spearheaded the creation of a community college along with provincial organizations for young people, parents, and the cultural sector. The institution and organizations in question were the Collège de l'Île, the Jeunesse acadienne et francophone de l'Île-du-Prince-Édouard, the Comité des parents francophones de l'Île-du-Prince-Édouard, and the Fédération culturelle acadienne de l'Île-du-Prince-Édouard. Over the years, the various local branches of the SSTA were gradually replaced by regional committees that became the prime movers for the establishment of school-community centres, the first of which was the Carrefour de l'Isle-Saint-Jean that opened in Charlottetown in 1991. There are now six school-community centres that serve all the francophones on the Island. They each constitute an important gathering place for activities in French in their respective regions.

In 1980, CBC/Radio-Canada installed a transmitter that enabled all Islanders to capture its television programs in French. Two years later, the same thing was done for its radio programs. In 1983, at the request of the SSTA, CBC/Radio-Canada created a radio program designed specifically for the francophone public on the Island, an initiative that helped strengthen the ties between all members of the French-speaking community. With the advent of the Internet and social media, opportunities for contacts between Acadians and francophones all over the world have increased immeasurably.

Special radio program on the occasion of the 5th anniversary of Radio-Canada's program *Bonjour Atlantique, édition Île-du-Prince-Édouard,* recorded at the Centre d'éducation Évangéline on October 21, 1991. Host Georges Arsenault interviewing J. Edmond Arsenault. (Georges Arsenault Collection)

A remarkable transformation has taken place in Prince Edward Island since 1970 with regard to the status of the French language and the Acadian culture. Although the number of Islanders with French as their first language diminished considerably during the 20th century, the French language has never been given so much prominence. Eloquent proof of this new standing is the *French Language Services Act*, promulgated in the year 2000 by the government of Prince Edward Island.

The pressure of assimilation will never subside, but federal and provincial laws ensure that the French language is better protected now than it ever was in the past. In addition, there has been a veritable rush on the part of anglophone parents to enrol their children in the French Immersion program. According to the 2016 federal census, 3.3 per cent of Islanders (4,665) declared that French was their first language spoken, whereas 12.7 per cent of Islanders (17,840) indicated that they had a knowledge of French.

Signing of the official proclamation of part of the *French Language Services Act* on March 3,2000. From left, Premier Pat Binns, SSTA president Antoine Richard and Mitch Murphy, Minister Responsible for Francophone Affairs. (Photo: *La Voix acadienne*)

The annual general meeting of Jeunesse acadienne in 1997. The association was founded in 1976. (Photo: *La Voix acadienne*)

Part of the Island delegation at the 22nd Final of the 2001 Jeux de l'Acadie held in the Evangeline Region. (Photo: *La Voix acadienne*)

Chapter 8

Social and Cultural Life

Like their compatriots in the neighbouring provinces, the Island Acadians inherited a rich oral and rural culture that permeated their daily life until the transformations brought on by the Second World War.

Before radio and television were commonplace in homes and before paved roads made travelling by car easier, the social and cultural activities of the majority of Islanders took place within the confines of their villages and parishes. Even if they were surrounded by people of different ethnic origins and religions, for a long time Acadians rarely married outside their own ethnic community. It was not until the mid-1800s that one started seeing mixed marriages, although they did not become more commonplace until the 1900s.

Consequently, for many years Acadian villages remained very close-knit communities. Entertainment took place in the home or sometimes in the local school that served as a community hall. Songs, folktales, and legends brought by ancestors from France were passed down from one generation to the next. Every village had at least one storyteller who went from house to house in the off-season to entertain people with his or her stories. There were also men and women who made it their duty to compose songs about amusing or tragic events that happened in their village.

Most of the festivities and celebrations were organized after the heavy farm work was finished and the fishermen had put away their boats for the winter. First, there were weddings that sometimes lasted for two days, bringing relatives and neighbours together for celebrations of dancing and an abundance of food. Frolics or bees were occasions when adults met for labour-intensive tasks like ploughing, barn building, and spinning wool. These gatherings provided excellent opportunities for socializing and amusement. They invariably ended with a good meal and often with music and dancing.

The feast days and holidays of the liturgical calendar helped brighten the long winter months. In addition to Christmas and New Year's Day, there was Epiphany on January 6 when people would get together to draw the favours in the *gâteau des Rois* (King Cake). A king and queen, chosen according to whose piece of cake contained the hidden favours, presided over an evening of party games, songs, and music. On February 2, Candlemas Day, a group of young men would follow a leader around their village to collect food for the poor. Some of the food was saved to make *râpure* or chicken *fricot* for a party that was held the same evening at one of the local homes.

Gathering at Evangeline Arsenault's parents' home in Urbainville on the occasion of her marriage to Mathurin Gallant on October 6, 1913. (Georges Arsenault Collection)

Shrovetide, the week before the beginning of Lent, was always full of festivities. People would dance and play cards most evenings, particularly on Shrove Monday and Shrove Tuesday (Mardi Gras). They also enjoyed good food before began those 40 days of fasting and abstinence imposed by the Catholic Church. On the fourth Thursday of Lent, to break the monotony of this long period of privation during which any form of amusement or revelry was forbidden, a person called the Mi-Carême would pay a visit. This was an adult disguised in strange and scary clothing who would distribute treats to good little boys and girls. In some

Pascal Poirier

Island Acadians have composed many ballads in memory of people who drowned. The oldest-known one is about Pascal Poirier, a man from Tignish who lost his life in 1837 when he was crossing the Northumberland Strait with his wife Marie Savoie, a native of Buctouche, New Brunswick. The following three verses are from the ballad sung in French by Marie-Anne Gallant, from St. Edward, and collected in 1976. The name of the person who composed the song is unknown.

Ah ! cet aimable Pascal qui demeure sur l'île Saint-Jean,
Épousait seconde femme, bien heureux et bien content.
Quelque temps s'a-t-écoulé, la belle dame elle s'ennuie,
Pour aller se consoler, elle demande à son mari :

Allons donc, cher mari, allons donc nous promener,
Allons donc sur la grand'terre voir nos parents et nos amis.
Cet homme si plein de complaisance, il prévoit pas le danger,
Il la met dans sa voiture, le mauvais temps s'a-t-élevé.

Ah ! cet aimable Pascal, voyant son épouse à l'eau,
Il s'écrie, il verse des larmes, et ça fut que des sanglots.
Mais malgré sa grande misère, il la tenait par un pied,
Malheureux sa destinée, elle se sauve, lui s'a néyé.

Oh! that kind Pascal who lived on Île Saint-Jean,
Married to his second wife, was very happy and content.
After some time passed, the lovely lady was lonesome.
To console herself, she said to her husband:

So let's go, my dear husband, let's go visiting,
So let's go to the mainland to see our friends and relatives.
Always anxious to please, this man saw no harm,
He put her in his boat, but bad weather sprung up.

Oh! that kind Pascal, seeing his wife in the water,
He yelled, he wept, and he sobbed.
Despite great difficulty, he managed to hold on to her foot,
His fate was sad, she was saved, and he drowned.

villages, a number of Mi-Carêmes would go around the community together in the evening making house calls. They carried sticks to scare away anyone who tried to take off their masks.

The Mi-Carême pays a visit to Maurice and Kathleen Poirier's house in Mill River in 1994. (Maurice et Kathleen Poirier Collection)

Happy Weddings

A double wedding took place in Rustico on February 7, 1893. The brides and grooms were Valentine Blanchard and Anselme Doucet and Marie Doucet and Eusèbe Gallant. One of their friends published an account of the wedding in the newspaper *L'Évangéline*. Here is a translation of part of the description.

> *Wedding parties always occasion much pleasure and entertainment. People who have the good fortune to attend enjoy talking about them, especially when they have spent a few very delightful days.* [...]
>
> *According to the Acadian custom, dancing started after a sumptuous breakfast and continued all day except for time devoted to delicious meals. We danced to the tunes of the fiddle played by Mr. Paul Poirier who, because of his skills and great reputation as a fiddler, reminds Acadians of Michael in the poem Evangeline. With baton in hand, Mr. Firmin Gallant chose the dancers who had to replace the ones on the floor; thanks to his capable direction, not a single person who wanted to dance was forgotten. Those who preferred to take part in the games, which had been obtained especially for the occasion, could enjoy the sound of the constant shuffle and movement of feet keeping time to the music of the fiddle.*
>
> *By nightfall all the guests had said good-bye to the newlyweds after once again wishing them happiness and prosperity.*
>
> *The next day, many of the friends gathered at the homes of Mr. Gallant and Mr. Moïse Blanchard to celebrate twice the happy wedding and another day was spent with considerable pleasure.*

Although a few of these traditions have survived in some Acadian communities, most of them disappeared over the years. Several families in West Prince, for example, still make sure Mi-Carême pays her annual visit to the young children. Shrovetide is still celebrated in the Evangeline Region with traditional music, molasses taffy, fudge, and the customary dishes made with grated potatoes.

Fisherman, carpenter, and singer, Eddy Arsenault (1921-2014), of Saint-Chrysostome, was one of the best and most influential fiddlers on the Island. (Photo: Georges Arsenault)

A Transformed Society

After the Second World War, profound changes took place in Island society. As elsewhere in the Maritimes, rural life was transformed. Most of the family farms disappeared, little village schools were replaced by regional schools, women entered the workplace in large numbers, and big families were no longer the norm. However, thanks to government programs aimed at modernizing and diversifying the economy, the standard of living and the well-being of the entire population was considerably improved. From a sociocultural point of view, the advent of television, at first only in English, had a major impact on the daily life of Islanders because it exposed them to a world that was predominantly American and English-speaking.

Needless to say, these winds of change also affected the Acadians. The closure of village schools accelerated the assimilation of their children who were forced to attend the consolidated anglophone schools. But, as we have explained in previous chapters, a movement took place in the 1960s that countered the trend towards anglicization and the weakening of the Acadian identity. A resurgence of pride emerged throughout the Acadian communities in the Maritimes and the French language was bolstered across Canada.

The opening of the Acadian Museum of Prince Edward Island in Miscouche in 1964 was one of the first efforts to conserve and promote the history and heritage of Island Acadians. That same year the Acadian community in Summerside launched its Mardi Gras festivities, which in subsequent years became an important cultural event in the town. In 1967, people in Mont-Carmel built the Acadian Pioneer Village (later renamed the Village de l'Acadie) where in 1971 the Étoile de Mer restaurant was opened: the first restaurant in the Maritime provinces to feature traditional Acadian dishes. Providing a showcase for Acadian musicians and songs in French, the first Acadian Festival of the Evangeline Region was inaugurated the same year.

Professor and historian J. Henri Blanchard and Sister Antoinette DesRoches at the official opening of the Acadian Museum of P.E.I. on August 25th, 1964. Sister DesRoches was the Museum's first director. (Acadian Museum of P.E.I. Collection)

Summerside Acadian fiddlers at the Mardi Gras festivities in 1979. From left, Ervin Saulnier, John Gauthier, and Toussaint Arsenault. (Photo: Georges Arsenault)

Thanks to the Saint Thomas Aquinas Society (SSTA) and the work of its cultural animation committee, a number of sociocultural organizations were formed, including the Centre culturel Port-Lajoie (1972) in Charlottetown and the Club Ti-Pa (1974) in the Tignish-Palmer Road area. Choirs, traditional dance troupes, and amateur theatre groups were also established. In 1990, the Fédération culturelle de l'Île-du-Prince-Édouard took over the cultural wing of the SSTA with the mandate to manage and support the cultural and artistic development of the Acadian and francophone community on the Island.

The Evangeline Dancers founded in 1976. (Photo: Georges Arsenault)

Numerous musicians contributed greatly to making Island Acadians better known not only throughout the province but also across Canada and abroad. This is particularly true in the case of songwriters and singers like Angèle Arsenault and Lennie Gallant, along with groups like Panou, Barachois, and Vishtèn who have all expressed their pride in belonging to the Acadian community.

Singer-songwriter Angèle Arsenault (1943-2014), from Abram-Village, was the Island's first professional Acadian singer.

Y'a une étoile pour vous is one of her best known songs.

Lennie Gallant, a native of Rustico, is recognized as one of Canada's leading singer-songwriters. (Photo: Daryll Thériault)

The popular supper theatre called *La Cuisine à Mémé*, which began in 1985 and took place in the summertime in the Village de l'Acadie in Mont-Carmel, gave many young Acadians their first experience as professional performers. A supper theatre called *V'nez chou nous* was created by the Club Ti-Pa in the West Prince region in 1990. The play, based on Acadian history and culture, was performed for many summers and enabled audiences to discover the wealth of local talent.

Members of the dinner theatre *V'nez chou nous* presenting the play *La parenté* in Tignish in 2001. (Photo: Georges Arsenault)

Aware of the lack of pedagogical resources related to Acadian history and culture, the SSTA launched a project in 1979 designed to fill the vacuum. A series of thematic booklets were produced under the direction of Georges Arsenault and subsequently published in book form in 1987 as *Les Acadiens de l'Île, 1720-1980.* The English translation by Sally Ross followed in 1989.

The media have played an important role in the promotion of Acadian culture. The weekly newspaper *La Voix acadienne*, established in 1976, has been very supportive of the Acadian and francophone artistic scene while at the same time featuring articles on various aspects of cultural heritage. Antoinette Gallant and Alice Richard, for example, both wrote stories in Acadian French chronicling daily life. Gallant's stories appeared regularly under the heading *Rustico on raconte* and Alice Richard's column was called *Pélagie et Henriette*.

Obviously attitudes have evolved considerably since the days when Acadian men and women chose to assimilate and hide their identity because they had been led to believe that "French was cheap" and that success was only measured in English. Mentalities progressed over the decades as the French language and the Acadian culture were gradually treated with greater respect. Whether you were an English-speaking or a French-speaking Acadian, you no longer felt embarrassed to say that you were "Acadian" or "French." The Acadian culture and the Acadian identity became a source of pride.

The **Miscouche Band** in 1929 under the direction of Arsène Poirier. Founded in 1889, the last version of this band played from 1991 to 2005. (Elmer Gaudet Collection)

Alma Buote (1894-1966), from Tignish, was the Island's first professional Acadian visual artist. (J. Henri Gaudet Collection, P.E.I. Acadian Research Centre)

Epilogue

The history of the Acadians of Prince Edward Island forms an important part not only of the history of Canada, but also of the evolution of the Canadian Francophonie. Over the course of three centuries, Island Acadians have faced innumerable challenges. The first French and Acadian families put down roots on the Island in 1720. Thirty-eight years later, almost all the Acadian and French inhabitants were deported from the Island or fled. The few families who managed to stay provided the thread for a continuous presence of the Acadian people in the Garden of the Gulf.

After many difficult years, the Acadian community on the Island gradually regained strength, but was nevertheless a cultural and linguistic minority in British territory. For a long time Acadians found themselves very low on the social scale. During the second half of the 19th century, this small French-speaking community began expanding its horizons socially, economically, and politically, which, of course, meant a certain amount of integration into the English-speaking majority. This resulted in such a strong trend towards assimilation that Senator Pascal Poirier, one of the prominent Acadian leaders in the Maritime provinces, said in 1907: "Nowhere in Acadie is the French sentiment more alive than on Île Saint-Jean; but nowhere is English spoken more often in the home, and that situation represents a significant threat to our people."

Pascal Poirier was right to have feared for the future of the French language on Prince Edward Island because today French is the mother tongue of only a small percentage of Islanders of Acadian descent. As we have pointed out, various factors, including mixed marriages, contributed to this language loss. This cultural intermingling began in the 1800s but has grown exponentially since the 1960s. A clear indication of this phenomenon is the high percentage of children with non-Acadian family names attending francophone schools in Prince Edward Island today. In fact, like the majority of Islanders, a large number of Acadians declare that they have more than one ethnic origin.

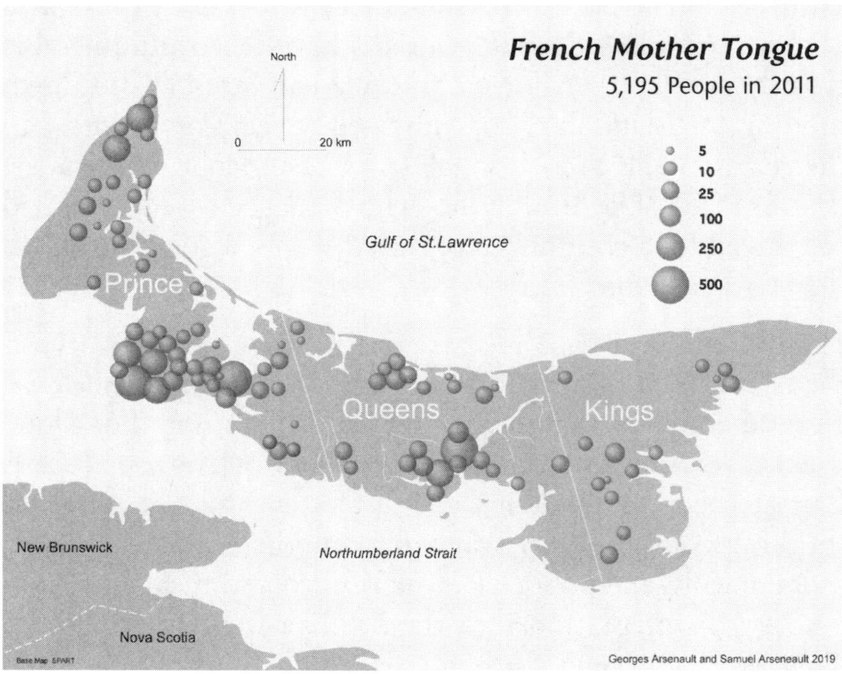

Until fairly recently many Acadians found that it was in their interest to have a family name that facilitated their integration into the dominant English-speaking British population. That is rarely considered necessary nowadays. People prefer more and more to assert and preserve their Acadian identity. Aware that the French language is the main cultural identifier, many parents have chosen to send their children to French schools.

The French-speaking community on Prince Edward Island has changed considerably since 1970. Before then, the vast majority of people who spoke French in the province were Acadians. Thanks to the arrival of numerous francophones from other parts of Canada and even other countries, the community is much more diverse today. Furthermore, the popularity of the French Immersion program in schools throughout the province has resulted in a steadily increasing number of anglophones who speak French as a second language.

The flourishing Acadian and francophone community today has benefited from generations of collective actions and accomplishments. Three hundred years after the arrival of the first French and Acadian settlers, Prince Edward Island has every reason to celebrate the survival and resilience of the French language and the Acadian culture.

From 1994 to 2003, the four musicians of **Barachois** promoted traditional Island Acadian music and songs throughout Canada, the United States, and several European countries. (Grady Poe Collection)

Bibliography

Bibliography containing the main volumes and articles consulted for this publication.

General

ARSENAULT, Georges. *The Island Acadians: 1720-1980.* Charlottetown: Ragweed Press, 1989, 296 p. Translated by Sally Ross.

BLANCHARD, J. Henri. *Acadiens de l'Ile-du-Prince-Edouard.* Charlottetown: Author, 1956, 144 p.

LAFOREST, Jacinthe and Georges ARSENAULT. *Acadian Women of Prince Edward Island: Three Centuries of Action.* Charlottetown: The Acorn Press, 2016, 193 p. Translated by Sally Ross.

Chapter I The Colony of Île Saint-Jean

ARSENAULT, Georges. "The Acadian Settlements of Pinette and Pointe Prime", *Keepsakes and Memories: Our Belfast,* Susan Hornby, editor. Belfast: Belfast Historical Society, 2009, pp. 23-37.

ARSENAULT, Georges. "The Malpeque Bay Acadians: 1728-1758", *The Island Magazine,* no. 66 (2009), pp. 2-9.

ARSENAULT, Georges. "Pierre Douville: un illustre fils de l'île Saint-Jean", *La Petite Souvenance,* no. 22 (2008), pp. 18-20. On line: http://museeacadien.org/lapetitesouvenance/?p=871, accessed October 17, 2018.

ARSENAULT, Georges. "Le premier insulaire d'origine européenne enterré à St. Peters Harbour", *La Petite Souvenance,* no. 16 (2002), pp. 9-11. On line: http://museeacadien.org/lapetitesouvenance/?p=668, accessed October 17, 2018.

HARVEY, D.C. *The French Régime in Prince Edward Island.* New York: AMS Press, 1970 (1st edition,Yale University Press, 1926), 265 p.

LOCKERBY, Earle. "Colonization of Île St.-Jean: Charting Today's Evangeline Region", *The Island Magazine*, no. 47 (2000), pp. 20-30.

LOCKERBY, Earle. "The Comte de Saint-Pierre and Ile Saint-Jean", *The Island Magazine,* no. 61 (2007), pp. 15-23.

LOCKERBY, Earle. "Discovering Local History Through Church Records of Saint-Pierre-du-Nord (1724-1758)", *La Petite Souvenance*, Number 17 (2003), pp. 19-26. On line: http://museeacadien.org/lapetitesouvenance/?p=713, accessed October 17, 2018.

LOCKERBY, Earle and Douglas SOBEY. *Samuel Holland. His Work and Legacy on Prince Edward Island*. Charlottetown: Island Studies Press, 2015, 273 p.

MACLEAN, Jill. *Jean Pierre Roma of the Company of the East of Isle St. Jean*. Charlottetown: The Acorn Press, 2005, 48 p.

Chapter 2 The Deportation

ARSENAULT, Georges. "L'île Saint-Jean et la Déportation de 1755", *La Petite Souvenance*, no. 19 (2005), pp. 12-13. On line: http://museeacadien.org/lapetitesouvenance/?p=811, accessed October 17, 2018.

ARSENAULT, Georges. "Le Grand Dérangement et les Acadiens de l'île Saint-Jean", *Lire du fragment: analyses et procédés littéraires*, Carlo Lavoie, editor. Montréal: Éditions Nota bene, 2008, pp. 21- 34.

ARSENAULT, Georges. "The Saga of Alexis Doiron", *The Island Magazine,* no. 39 (1996), pp. 12-18.

LEBLANC, Ronnie-Gilles, editor. *Du Grand Dérangement à la Déportation. Nouvelles perspectives historiques*. Moncton: Chaire d'études acadiennes, Université de Moncton, 2005, 466 p.

LOCKERBY, Earle. *Deportation of the Prince Edward Island Acadians*. Montréal: Éditions au Carré, 2008, 112 p.

Chapter 3 Returning to Île Saint-Jean

ARSENAULT, Georges. "Les Acadiens de la baie de Malpèque: 1720-1820", *Les Cahiers de la Société historique acadienne*, vol. 39, nos. 2 and 3 (2008), pp. 56-121.

ARSENAULT, Georges and Earle LOCKERBY. "The Acadians on Saint-John's Island in the 1760s", *The Island Magazine*, no. 79 (2016), pp. 12-25.

ARSENAULT, Jean-Paul. 'The Odyssey of Joseph 'Chaculot' Gaudet and Marie-Blanche Bourg", *The Island Magazine*, no. 54 (2003), pp. 11-15

Chapter 4 Economic Life

ARSENAULT, Georges. *Les Acadiens de Summerside / The Acadians of Summerside.* Tracadie-Sheila: La Grande Marée, 2013, 221 p.

ARSENAULT, Georges. *L'Agriculture chez les Acadiens de l'Île-du-Prince-Édouard 1720-1980.* Summerside: SSTA, 1981, 69 p.

ARSENAULT, Georges. "La colonisation et les Acadiens de l'Île-du-Prince-Édouard à l'époque des premières Conventions nationales acadiennes", *Les Cahiers de la Société historique acadienne,* vol. 16, no. 1 (1985), pp. 19-30.

ARSENAULT, Georges. "Comment des pauvres gens peuvent devenir banquiers? Extrait d'une lettre du père Georges-Antoine Belcourt, curé de Rustico", *La Petite Souvenance,* no. 18 (2004), pp. 18-19. On line: http://museeacadien.org/lapetitesouvenance/?p=767, accessed October 17, 2018.

ARSENAULT, Georges. "DesRoches, Gilbert", in *Dictionary of Canadian Biography*, vol. 14, University of Toronto / Université Laval, 2003–, accessed November 1, 2018, http://www.biographi.ca/en/bio/desroches_gilbert_14E.html.

ARSENAULT, Georges. "Gallant, Joseph", in *Dictionary of Canadian Biography*, vol. 15, University of Toronto/Université Laval, 2003–, accessed November 1, 2018, http://www.biographi.ca/en/bio/gallant_joseph_15E.html.

ARSENAULT, Georges. *Histoire de l'émigration chez les Acadiens de l'Île-du-Prince-Édouard.* Summerside: SSTA, 1980, 42 p.

ARSENAULT, Georges. "Instinct for Business. Pioneer Acadian Entrepreneurs on Prince Edward Island", *The Island Magazine*, no. 51 (2002), pp. 24-30.

ARSENAULT, Georges and Cécile Gallant. *Histoire de la pêche chez les Acadiens de l'Île-du-Prince-Édouard.* Summerside: SSTA, 1980, 52 p.

BERTRAND, Gabriel. *Paroisse acadienne de Rustico (Î.-P.-É.) et la Banque des fermiers. Recueil de citations épistolaires du père Georges-Antoine Belcourt.* Moncton: Chaire d'études coopératives, Université de Moncton, 1995, 101 p. On line: http://www.umoncton.ca/umcm-ccpagc/files/umcm-ccpagc/wf/wf/pdf/cahier%20G.Bertrand.pdf, accessed November 1, 2018.

CLARK, A.H. *Three Centuries and the Island, A Historical Geography of Settlement and Agriculture in Prince Edward Island, Canada.* Toronto: University of Toronto Press, 1959, 287 p.

GALLANT, Cécile. *Le Mouvement coopératif chez les Acadiens de la région Évangéline (1862-1982).* Wellington: Le Conseil coopératif de l'Île-du-Prince-Édouard, 1982, 283 p.

Chapter 5 The Catholic Church and Religious Life

ARSENAULT, Georges. *La Religion et les Acadiens à l'Île-du-Prince-Édouard 1720-1980.* Summerside: SSTA, 1983, 102 p.

ARSENAULT, Georges. "Arsenault, Pierre-Paul", in *Dictionary of Canadian Biography*, vol. 15, University of Toronto/Université Laval, 2003–, accessed November 1, 2018, http://www.biographi.ca/en/bio/arsenault_pierre_paul_15E.html.

BLANCHARD, Francis-C. "Perrey, Syvain-Éphrem", in *Dictionary of Canadian Biography*, vol. 11, University of Toronto/Université Laval, 2003–, accessed November 1, 2018, http://www.biographi.ca/en/bio/perrey_sylvain_ephrem_11E.html.

GALLANT, Cécile. "L'engagement social de Georges-Antoine Belcourt, curé de Rustico, 1859-1869", *Les Cahiers de la Société historique acadienne,* vol. 11, no. 4 (1985), pp. 316-339.

PINEAU, Wilfred. *Le Clergé français dans l'Île du Prince-Édouard, 1721-1821.* Québec: Les Éditions Ferland, 1967, 157 p.

STANLEY, George F.G. "Ce prêtre difficile. Commentaires sur les activités du Père Georges-Antoine Belcourt", *Les Cahiers de la Société historique acadienne,* vol.14, no. 2, 1983, pp. 39-58.

Chapter 6 Education

ARSENAULT, Georges. *L'Éducation chez les Acadiens de l'Île-du-Prince-Édouard 1720-1980.* Summerside: SSTA, 1982, 85 p.

ARSENAULT, Georges. "La naissance de l'École Évangéline", *École Évangéline, 50 ans déjà. Le Grand Rassemblement.* Abram-Village: École Évangéline, 2011, pp. 3-6.

BLANCHARD, Francis C. "Arsenault, Joseph-Octave (1866-1918)", in *Dictionary of Canadian Biography,* vol. 14, University of Toronto/Université Laval, 2003–, accessed November 1, 2018, http://www.biographi.ca/en/bio/arsenault_joseph_octave_1866_1918_14E.html.

LA PETITE SOUVENANCE, No. 20 (2006), 44 p. Number dedicated to J. Henri Blanchard. On line: http://museeacadien.org/lapetitesouvenance/?cat=8, accessed October 17, 2018.

Chapter 7 Living in French

ARSENAULT, Georges. "The Acadian Experience in Prince Edward Island", *Les Cahiers de la Société historique acadienne,* vol. 14, no. 2 (1983), pp. 59-72.

ARSENAULT, Georges. "Buote, Gilbert", in *Dictionary of Canadian Biography,* vol. 13, University of Toronto/Université Laval, 2003–, accessed November 1, 2018, http://www.biographi.ca/en/bio/buote_gilbert_13E.html.

ARSENAULT, Georges. "Le dilemme des Acadiens de l'Île-du-Prince-Édouard au 19e siècle", *Acadiensis*, vol. XIV, no. 2 (1985), pp. 29-45. On line: https://journals.lib.unb.ca/index.php/acadiensis/article/view/12064/12908, accessed November 1, 2018.

ARSENAULT, Georges. "The Miscouche Convention, 1884", *The Island Magazine*, no. 15 (1984), pp. 14-19.

ARSENAULT, Georges and Jacinthe LAFOREST. *Livre-souvenir, La Société Saint-Thomas-d'Aquin, 1919-1994*, Summerside: SSTA, 1994, 93 p.

BASQUE, Maurice (in collaboration with Eric Snow). *La Société nationale de l'Acadie. Au coeur de la réussite d'un peuple.* Moncton: Les Éditions de la Francophonie, 2006, 265 p.

LA PETITE SOUVENANCE, no. 10 : "Un peuple à unir" (special number on the occasion of the centennial of the Acadian flag), 1984, 32 p. On line: http://museeacadien.org/lapetitesouvenance/?cat=3, accessed October 17, 2018.

Chapter 8 Social and Cultural Life

ARSENAULT, Georges. "Antoinette Gallant, raconteuse par excellence", *La Petite Souvenance*, no. 17 (2003), pp. 4-9. On line: http://museeacadien.org/lapetitesouvenance/?p=699, accessed October 17, 2018.

ARSENAULT, Georges. Cent ans de succès / A Century of Success., L'Exposition agricole et le Festival acadien de la région Évangéline: Wellington, 2002, 86 p.

ARSENAULT, Georges. *Complaintes acadiennes de l'Île-du-Prince-Édouard.* Montréal: Leméac, 1980, 261 p.

ARSENAULT, Georges. *Acadian Legends, Folktales, and Songs from Prince Edward Island.* Charlottetown: The Acorn Press, 2002, 158 p. Translated by Sally Ross.

ARSENAULT, Georges. *Acadian Traditions on Candlemas Day: Candles, Pancakes, and House Visits.* Charlottetown: The Acorn Press, 2012, 143 p. Translated by Sally Ross.

ARSENAULT, Georges. "Le gâteau des Rois: Twelfth Night Celebrations in Acadian Prince Edward Island", *The Island Magazine*, no. 20 (1986), pp. 23-28.

ARSENAULT, Georges. *Acadian Mi-Carême. Masks and Merrymaking.* Charlottetown: The Acorn Press, 2009, 164 p. Translated by Sally Ross.

ARSENAULT, Georges. *Acadian Christmas Traditions.* Charlottetown: The Acorn Press, 2007, 160 p. Translated by Sally Ross.

ARSENAULT, Georges. *Par un dimanche au soir : Léah Maddix, chanteuse et conteuse acadienne.* Moncton: Éditions d'Acadie, 1993, 188 p.

ARSENAULT, Georges. "Le Père Pierre-Paul Arsenault : un pionnier en folklore acadien", *Les Cahiers de la Société historique acadienne,* vol. 27, no. 1 (1996), pp. 19-32

ARSENAULT, Georges. "Les pique-niques paroissiaux acadiens à l'Île-du-Prince-Édouard au 19e et au début de 20e siècle", *Les Cahiers de la Société historique acadienne*, vol. 48, nos. 3 and 4, 2017, pp. 77-95.

Miscellaneous

ARSENAULT, A.E. *Memoirs of the Hon. A.E. Arsenault.* [Charlottetown: Author, 1951], 188 p.

ARSENAULT, Georges. "The Acadians in Island Politics", *The Island Magazine,* no. 43 (1998), pp. 13-22.

ARSENAULT, Georges. "Le Sénateur Joseph Octave Arsenault", *The Island Magazine*, no. 33 (1993), pp. 25-29.

ARSENAULT, Georges. "Perry, Stanislaus Francis", in *Dictionary of Canadian Biography*, vol. 12, University of Toronto/Université Laval, 2003–, accessed November 1, 2018, http://www.biographi.ca/en/bio/perry_stanislaus_francis_12E.html.

Acknowledgements

I would like to express my sincerest thanks to all the individuals and institutions who, in one way or another, helped bring this book to fruition. First of all, I am particularly indebted to my friends Francine Desmeules, Daniel Masson, and Sally Ross who kindly read, corrected, and annotated the original French manuscript.

I would also like to thank the geographer Samuel Arsenault who produced the maps, the artist Réjean Roy who created the evocative drawings, and the artist Noëlla Richard who gave me permission to use her painting inspired by the Acadian flag for the cover of this book.

My warmest thanks also to *La Voix acadienne*, the Acadian Museum of Prince Edward Island and its Research Centre, and the Public Archives and Records Office of Prince Edward Island that provided a number of photos. Many thanks also to all the individuals who let me use photos from their private collections.

I wish to acknowledge with gratitude the financial support of the Prince Edward Island Museum and Heritage Foundation.

And, finally, my sincere thanks to Sally Ross who translated this book, to Elizabeth Eve who edited the translation, to the graphic designer Guy Vaillancourt for his patience and dedication, and to Terrilee Bulger, the owner of Acorn Press, who kindly accepted to publish this book.

Georges Arsenault

Books by Georges Arsenault

Complaintes acadiennes de l'Île-du-Prince-Édouard. Montréal: Leméac, 1980.

Courir la Chandeleur. Moncton: Éditions d'Acadie, 1982.

Les Acadiens de l'Île : 1720-1980. Moncton: Éditions d'Acadie, 1987.

The Island Acadians: 1720-1980. Charlottetown: Ragweed Press, 1989. Translated by Sally Ross.

Par un dimanche au soir : Léah Maddix, chanteuse et conteuse acadienne. Moncton: Éditions d'Acadie, 1993.

Guide historique de la région Évangéline. Moncton: self-published, 1994.

Historical Guidebook of the Evangeline Region. Charlottetown: self-published, 1998. Translated by Sally Ross.

Contes, légendes et chansons de l'Île-du-Prince-Édouard. Moncton: Éditions d'Acadie, 1998.

Acadian Legends, Folktales, and Songs from Prince Edward Island. Charlottetown: The Acorn Press, 2002. Translated by Sally Ross.

Cent ans de succès / A Century of Success. Wellington: L'Exposition agricole et le Festival acadien de la région Évangéline, 2002. Translated by Daphne Davey.

Noël en Acadie. Tracadie-Sheila: La Grande Marée, 2005.

Acadian Christmas Traditions. Charlottetown: The Acorn Press, 2007. Translated by Sally Ross.

La Mi-Carême en Acadie. Tracadie-Sheila: La Grande Marée, 2008.

Acadian Mi-Carême: Masks and Merrymaking. Charlottetown: The Acorn Press, 2009. Translated by Sally Ross.

La Chandeleur en Acadie. Tracadie-Sheila: La Grande Marée, 2011.

Acadian Traditions on Candlemas Day: Pancakes, and House Visits. Charlottetown, The Acorn Press, 2012. Translation by Sally Ross.

Les Acadiennes de l'Île-du-Prince-Édouard : trois siècles d'action. Summerside: Actions Femmes Î.-P.-É., 2011. Co-authored with Jacinthe Laforest.

La Roche & Grand Ruisseau: An Illustrated History of Egmont Bay and Mont-Carmel. Tracadie-Sheila: La Grande Marée, 2012.

Les Acadiens de Summerside / The Acadians of Summerside. Tracadie-Sheila: La Grande Marée, 2013.

Acadian Women of Prince Edward Island. Charlottetown: The Acorn Press, 2016. Co-authored with Jacinthe Laforest, translated by Sally Ross.

Contes, légendes et chansons de l'Île-du-Prince-Édouard. Second edition. Tracadie: La Grande Marée, 2018.